Time After Time

A Farm to Table
Culinary Journey

Using Flavored Olive Oils and Balsamic Vinegars

Michele Castellano Senac

There Are Diamonds In The Sky

To Clare

my favorite Master Chef

Photography by Lorrie Castellano

ISBN: 978-0-692-55007-6

First Edition

Other books by the author

Around the Table, A Culinary Memoir by Two Sisters
by Michele Castellano Senac and Lorrie Castellano

As Old As Time: A Culinary Odyssey Using Flavored Olive Oils and Balsamic Vinegars

CONTENTS

Pasta

Potatoes, Rice and Grains

Meat

Seafood

INTRODUCTION

When I was growing up my mother prepared and served fresh vegetables and salads at every meal. Fresh fruit was readily available, according to the season. As a child, it was a treat to sit at the kitchen table and watch my Grandma Castellano lovingly peel an apple, slicing it carefully and precisely so the slice would fit into my hand for easy nibbling.

I learned the importance of healthy eating from my mother long before it was mainstream. Her love of olive oil and balsamic vinegar was legend in our family, and she passed that love onto me. My mother used olive oil for everything. She purchased the best, freshest quality olive oil that the budget would allow. Her meals were simple, delicious and nutritious. I have been blessed to come from a long line of good cooks, including my grandmothers and aunts, who understood the importance of a healthy, fresh diet.

My Grandpa Cibella planted and tended a garden his entire life up until a few days before he died at age 97. His tiny plot produced a harvest of tomatoes, basil, parsley, sweet and hot peppers, and other vegetables. I learned early on how tasty garden-fresh foods are.

A few years ago I was drawn to an olive oil store near my home. It was there, first as a customer and then as an employee, that I tasted a variety of Extra-virgin Olive Oils, flavored Olive Oils and Dark and White Balsamic Vinegars. Finally there was a place to taste and purchase high quality Olive Oils and Balsamic Vinegars. This reinforced what I learned as a child about healthy eating, and it was the inspiration to write my second book, *As Old As Time, a Culinary Journey Using Flavored Olive Oils and Balsamic Vinegars.*

Growing your own food might not be an option or an interest. Today fresh vegetables, fruits, dairy, meats and poultry are available at local Farmer's Markets, community gardens, and many supermarkets. Purchasing high quality Olive Oils and Balsamic Vinegars is made easy by visiting your local olive oil store.

This book invites the reader to experience delicious farm to table foods prepared with Extra-virgin Olive Oils, flavored Olive Oils, and Dark and White Balsamic Vinegars. Join me in a Farm-to-Table Culinary Journey that *Time After Time* has proven to provide healthy, delicious, beautiful and satisfying meals.

Michele Castellano Senac

ABOUT THE FARM TO TABLE MOVEMENT

In times past, many grew their own fruits and vegetables and raised their own livestock. The Industrial Revolution in the late 1800s began to change that causing some to leave the farms for factory and city jobs. Transportation technology and agri-business increased and food began being shipped to locations farther and farther away from the places where it was grown. Because of this fresh fruits and vegetables had to be picked before they fully ripened and had absorbed nutrients. Rather than food grown for taste, the emphasis shifted to food that was resilient to long travel. Processed foods became available to save time in meal preparations. As a result, health and nutrition were compromised for the sake of convenience.

RETURNING TO OUR ROOTS

Many credit Alice Waters, who founded Chez Panisse in Berkeley, California in 1971, as the pioneer in the Farm to Table movement. Waters believed that cooking should be based on the finest, freshest seasonal ingredients that are produced sustainably and locally. Since then many similar restaurants have opened all over the country and the Farm to Table movement has flourished.

As the demand for fresh local produce grew, so did support of local farmers. Today Farmer's Markets are numerous in most locales, community gardens and home gardens are increasing, and food co-ops are becoming more popular.

HEALTH, PERSONAL AND ENVIRONMENTAL BENEFITS

The Farm To Table movement emphasizes simply prepared food comprised of locally sourced, seasonal ingredients. When food is grown locally, the local economy is helped and small farms are supported. By supporting local farmers, consumers contribute to the quality of life in their area. Since locally grown foods do not have to be shipped, produce can be picked when ripe and brought to market immediately. This preserves the taste and nutritional value. Fewer transport miles means fewer vehicle emissions and greenhouse gases, thereby helping the environment.

Knowing where the food we eat has been grown has physical and emotional benefits. Growing your own food has its own personal rewards of nurturing the growing process, harvesting, cooking, and bringing homegrown foods to your table. Purchasing vegetables, dairy, meat or poultry from a local farmer builds a relationship among you, the food and the grower. Eating seasonally helps keep the body in balance and in tune with the earth's natural cycles. Fresh grown food simply tastes better, retains more nutritional value and gives the body what it needs.

ABOUT EXTRA-VIRGIN OLIVE OILS AND BALSAMIC VINEGARS

Olive Oil and Balsamic Vinegar have a long, rich history. They have been part of our diets since records were kept and are included in many ancient texts, including the Bible, Torah and Koran. Many of the historical texts noted that the olive tree was sacred. The ancients used olive oil for cooking, lighting lamps, anointing, consecrating and for healing.

Balsamic Vinegar has been held in high regard for eons. As early as the first millennium it was mentioned as a health tonic, a remedy to plague, and to ward off evil spirits. The making of balsamic vinegar is shrouded in secrecy, even today.

Fortunately there is a considerable amount of information about Olive Oil and Balsamic Vinegar now available. Olive crush dates, the variety of olive and the country of origin are provided. With the number of specialty shops popping up, tasting before purchase is easy. The polyphenol count, which is a measure of anti-oxidants reflecting the health benefits of olive oil, is available for many olive oils.

With Balsamic Vinegar age is important in the taste and quality. Tasting a variety of aged balsamic vinegars gives the consumer first-hand knowledge and appreciation of the quality. Pairing Olive Oil and Balsamic Vinegar together is a natural fit that creates tasty combinations for salads, meats, fish, poultry and vegetables. Using good quality Olive Oil and Balsamic Vinegar in cooking is the perfect accompaniment to fresh foods, and adds to health and vitality.

Simply put, buy the Olive Oil and Balsamic Vinegar that pleases your palate and pocketbook. Be sure the Olive Oil is fresh and the Balsamic Vinegar is aged. You will be rewarded with great tasting, healthy meals.

SUMMARY OF HEALTH BENEFITS OF OLIVE OIL

* Heart healthy – prevents formation of LDL cholesterol, which is considered the "bad" cholesterol

* Helps control blood pressure, reducing the risks of stroke and heart attack

* Inhibits growth of some cancers because of its high antioxidant properties

* Helps control blood sugar and triglycerides

* Reduces severity of arthritis, asthma, psoriasis and eczema because of its natural anti-inflammatory properties

✳ Benefits the stomach by lowering hydrochloric acid levels

✳ Benefits hair and scalp by hydrating hair follicles, resulting in reduced hair loss and dandruff

✳ Moisturizes skin, nails and cuticles

SUMMARY OF HEALTH BENEFITS OF BALSAMIC VINEGAR

✳ Decreases the risk of heart attack by helping to normalize blood pressure and stabilize cholesterol levels

✳ Helps with weight stabilization and diabetes control due to its low glycemic scale, low calorie, sugar and carbohydrate content

✳ Helps fight cancer due to its bioflavonoid and antioxidant content

✳ Helps the digestive process by stimulating the pepsin enzyme which enhances the absorption of amino acids

✳ Supports bone health because it contains acetic acid and pepsin which help in the absorption of calcium and magnesium

✳ Helps with pain relief due to its anti-viral and anti-microbial properties

SMALL BITES

FARMSTEAD CHEESE
AND CRACKERS 12

7
SWEET-
SAVORY
SHRIMP
CEVICHE

4 HERB-SPIKED SPREAD

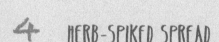

10

CLASSIC TUSCAN
BRUSCHETTA

WATERMELON
WONDER

8

FANCY GRILLED
CHERRY TOMATOES 2

FANCY GRILLED CHERRY TOMATOES

When tomatoes come into season, celebrate! There are so many ways to enjoy these bite-size delights. Eat alone as a snack, or slice in half and toss in a salad. Grilling them brings out their flavor, and combining them with rosemary and feta cheese creates the perfect starter or appetizer. The addition of flavored olive oil makes this a magnificent little treat.

Serves: 4

INGREDIENTS

1 pound cherry tomatoes

10 fresh rosemary stems, about 5 inches long, for skewers

½ pound feta cheese, cubed into 1-inch pieces

2 tablespoons fresh lemon juice

4 tablespoons Rosemary Olive Oil

Salt and pepper to taste

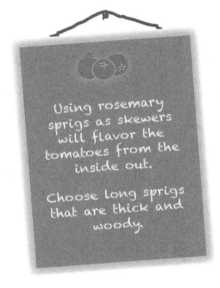

Using rosemary sprigs as skewers will flavor the tomatoes from the inside out.

Choose long sprigs that are thick and woody.

METHOD

Metal skewers can be used, but for an intense flavor, use rosemary stems. Strip the rosemary stems of leaves, being careful to leave just a few at the very top of the stem. Chop 2 teaspoons of the leaves and set aside.

In a small bowl, combine cubed cheese, 2 tablespoons of Rosemary Olive Oil, fresh rosemary and salt. Stir well and set aside.

Fire up the grill to a medium fire and oil the grill rack. Or heat the broiler to high.

Thread 4–6 tomatoes on each rosemary skewer, depending on the length of the skewer. Brush tomatoes with remaining Rosemary Olive Oil and sprinkle with salt and pepper.

Place on grill for about 2 minutes on each side, watching carefully until the tomatoes are just beginning to brown and split, turning gently. If using the broiler,

allow to broil on high for about 1–2 minutes until you see the tomatoes are getting soft and browning.

When tomatoes are ready, remove from skewers, adding them to the marinated cheese. Mix gently.

TO SERVE

Place in serving bowl. Garnish with any remaining rosemary leaves and serve with crackers, grilled pita or bread.

VARIATIONS

🐚 Both the marinated cheese and tomatoes could be served separately.

🐚 Use other flavored olive oils, such as Lemon, Herbes de Provence, Garlic, Chipotle, Basil, Tarragon, Tuscan Herb or Cilantro and Roasted Onion.

HERB-SPIKED SPREAD

This is an easily put-together spread that's healthy, tasty and makes a colorful presentation. Serve it with your choice of sliced veggies, rolled in lettuce leaves or with crackers, pita bread or grilled bread. Add a bowl of olives, preferably those lively green Castelventranos, and you've practically got a meal.

Makes 1¼ cup

INGREDIENTS

6 ounces goat cheese

½ cup fresh flat-leaf parsley, finely chopped

¼ cup fresh mint, finely chopped

2 tablespoons fresh dill, finely chopped

Drizzle of Dill Olive Oil

Water to thin, approximately 3 tablespoons

Salt and pepper to taste

Great tasting goat cheese is becoming readily available as more local farmers are raising goats and making cheese.

Look for goat cheese at the Farmer's Market or in the grocery store. It is also known as chevre.

METHOD

Place chopped parsley, mint, dill, salt and pepper in a medium bowl and mix.

In a food processor, blend cheese and add a little water for a smooth consistency. Add cheese to herbs and mix well, adding a drizzle of Dill Olive Oil. Mix again.

If you don't want to use a food processor, a hand masher or fork will also give a similar result.

TO SERVE

Place in colorful serving bowl or plate, drizzle with a little more Dill Olive Oil, and garnish with one or more remaining herbs and serve.

VARIATIONS

✎ Try using other flavored olive oils such as Garlic, Basil, Mushroom and Sage, or Herbes de Provence. A robust Extra-virgin Olive Oil also works well with this spread.

🧀 Feta, ricotta, cream cheese, queso fresco or any other soft cheese can be used instead of goat cheese.

SWEET-SAVORY SHRIMP CEVICHE

The combination of seafood, avocado and mangos is practically irresistible. Place a scoop on a tortilla or pita chip for a bite-size treat. Mix this in a salad, making it a perfectly refreshing lunch. Instead of shrimp a white, flaky fish can be used.

Serves: 4

INGREDIENTS

12 medium shrimp, deveined, tails removed, cooked and chopped

1 large avocado, chopped in small cubes

2 tablespoons Lime Olive Oil

2 limes, juiced to about 2 tablespoons, the remainder sliced for garnish

1 medium mango, chopped in small cubes

2 small tomatillos, finely chopped

1 small jalapeño, seeded, finely chopped

¼ cup red onion, finely chopped

2 tablespoons fresh cilantro, finely chopped

Salt and pepper to taste

METHOD

Place chopped avocado, Lime Olive Oil and lime juice in a bowl and gently stir. Add remainder of ingredients and gently combine.

TO SERVE

Place in colorful bowl and serve with chips of your choice.

VARIATIONS

🍤 Flavored olive oils are perfect for this dish. Try Lemon, Blood Orange, Basil, Cilantro and Roasted Onion or Tuscan Herb Olive Oils. To add heat, use Harissa, Green Chili or Chipotle Olive Oils.

WATERMELON WONDER

For a quick starter try this easy watermelon with balsamic syrup. Serve it with a cool glass of rosé wine and you have a memorable appetizer on a warm evening. This is also a great dessert.

Serves: 4–6

INGREDIENTS

½ medium seedless watermelon, cut in small wedges

¼ cup Traditional Dark Balsamic Vinegar

1 tablespoon sugar

6–8 fresh mint leaves, chopped, with a few leaves for garnish

METHOD

Combine Traditional Dark Balsamic Vinegar and sugar in a non-reactive saucepan, such as a stainless steel pan. Simmer over medium heat until thickened, stirring frequently, for about 10 minutes. Let cool to room temperature.

Slice watermelon into small wedges. Place on serving platter or individual serving plates.

Look for a sweet, seedless watermelon, such as Sugar Baby, at the Farmer's Market.

TO SERVE

Drizzle cooled balsamic syrup over watermelon slices. Top with chopped mint, and garnish with mint leaves.

VARIATIONS

✎ Try a flavored Dark Balsamic Vinegar syrup, such as Strawberry, Raspberry, Dark Cherry, Fig, Blueberry or Champagne.

🍃 Other melons in season also work well in this recipe.

CLASSIC TUSCAN BRUSCHETTA

In Italy bruschetta is served as a starter and usually consists of grilled bread that has been rubbed with garlic and then drizzled with olive oil and salt. It is often served to taste the very first olive oil of the season. There are a variety of toppings that are also used, including tomatoes, vegetables, beans, cured meats, and cheeses.

Serves: 2–3 slices per person

INGREDIENTS

1 loaf of Italian or French bread, thickly sliced

¼ cup Extra-Virgin Olive Oil

3–4 cloves garlic, peeled and smashed

4–5 tomatoes

10–12 basil leaves, sliced in thin strips, plus whole leaves for garnish

Salt, coarsely ground, to taste

Traditional Dark Balsamic Vinegar – a splash

This recipe is sure to please, especially when tomatoes are in season.

And when they're not, try most any other topping to create a pretty and delicious appetizer.

METHOD

Grill sliced bread or place in a grill pan on medium-high heat until crisp and brown. Or place bread under broiler for 1–2 minutes on each side. Take the smashed garlic and rub all over one side of each slice of bread, then drizzle about half the olive oil on the bread. You can also use a brush to coat the bread. Add a sprinkle of salt to each piece. Set aside.

Place chopped or sliced tomatoes and basil on bread, drizzle remaining Extra-virgin Olive Oil on the slices, top with basil strips and a little sprinkle of salt.

TO SERVE

Place toasts on serving platter. Garnish with basil leaves. Drizzle with Traditional Dark Balsamic Vinegar and serve.

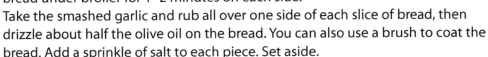

VARIATIONS

The possibilities are endless.

⚜ You can use Rosemary, Tuscan Herb, Garlic, Basil, Cilantro and Roasted Onion, Herbes de Provence, Green Chili or Harissa Olive Oil.

🫒 A drizzle of flavored Balsamic Vinegar using Strawberry, Fig, Sicilian Lemon, or Oregano Balsamic Vinegar will add another layer of flavor to this traditional favorite.

🍆 Instead of tomatoes, top the bread with prepared roasted red peppers, pesto, eggplant or artichoke spreads, cured sliced meats, anchovies or sardines.

FARMSTEAD CHEESE AND CRACKERS

Cheese and crackers are an easy go-to when you need a quick appetizer or small bite. The most popular local cheeses are usually made from cows or goats, but in some locales, sheep and buffalo cheese are available. Visit your local cheese maker at the farm or the Farmer's Market and ask for suggestions for a good, soft cheese to serve.

Serves: 4–6

INGREDIENTS

¾–1 pound local cheese

½ cup Dark Balsamic Vinegar

> Look for local artisan, farmstead and specialty cheese makers where you live.

METHOD

Pre-heat oven to 350°. Place cheese in a small baking pan and heat for about 5–10 minutes or until cheese is soft.

TO SERVE

Place cheese on serving dish and drizzle with Dark Balsamic Vinegar. Serve with crackers, warm bread rounds or pita bread.

VARIATIONS

- Many Dark Balsamic Vinegars pair well with cheese. Drizzle Raspberry, Strawberry, Blueberry, Tahitian Vanilla, Fig, Dark Espresso, Dark Chocolate, Lavender, Pomegranate or Champagne Balsamic Vinegar for a tasty and appetizing presentation.

- If time permits, making a Dark Balsamic Vinegar reduction, recipe on page 22, will add richness to the flavor.

- Dried fruit, such as cherries, raisins or apricots add color and flavor.

- Sprinkle nuts, such as chopped walnuts, almonds, or pecans, for texture and taste.

DRESSINGS, DRIZZLES & REDUCTIONS

ALL THE DRIZZLE
YOU'LL EVER NEED   20

14

VINAIGRETTE
101

17

FAVORITE FRUITY
DRESSING

TANGY BALSAMIC
SYRUP   16

BALSAMIC VINEGAR
REDUCTION 101   22

18   ZESTY GREEN DRIZZLE

VINAIGRETTE 101

Everyone loves a good salad dressing. And with so many great olive oils and balsamic vinegars from which to choose, selecting pairings can be intimidating. Consult the Pairings Section in Part Three for many tried and true options.

The magic ratio of Olive Oil to Balsamic Vinegar is 3 parts Olive Oil to 1 part Balsamic Vinegar. Whether you mix your vinaigrette in a blender, whisk it in a bowl or a glass, or put it in a mason jar and shake it like I do, using this ratio and mixing it well will result in an excellent dressing.

Here's a basic recipe that can be put together in no time.

Serves: 4–6

INGREDIENTS

¾ cup Extra-Virgin Olive Oil

¼ cup Dark or White Balsamic Vinegar

1 large clove garlic, smashed

½ teaspoon honey

½ teaspoon Dijon mustard

½ teaspoon salt, plus a sprinkle for the bowl

⅛ teaspoon pepper

METHOD

Peel and smash garlic. Put all ingredients in a glass jar and shake vigorously to blend well.

TO SERVE

Pour the desired amount of dressing in a large bowl and coat the bowl as evenly as you can with salad dressing. Then lightly sprinkle salt around the sides and bottom of the bowl.

Add salad greens of your choice and gently mix thoroughly. By "dressing the bowl" first, the vinaigrette is more evenly distributed and the salad greens are easily lightly coated.

VARIATIONS

🌿 Use the Pairings Section and choose your desired pairings of flavored Olive Oils and Balsamic Vinegars.

🍃 Try Lime or Lemon Olive Oil and consult the Pairings Section for a variety of White and Dark Balsamic Vinegar suggestions.

TANGY BALSAMIC SYRUP

This simple syrup is easy to make and has a variety of uses. Adding a bit of sugar increases the sweetness, giving it a sweet-sharp flavor so a little of this yummy syrup goes a long way.

Makes ¼ cup

INGREDIENTS

⅔ cup Traditional Dark Balsamic Vinegar

1 tablespoon dark brown sugar, packed

METHOD

In a non-reactive saucepan, such as stainless steel, combine sugar and Traditional Dark Balsamic Vinegar. Boil over medium heat for about 3–4 minutes, stirring using a wooden spatula. It is ready when it's thickened and syrupy and coats the back of a spoon.

You can store this simple syrup in a sealed jar or container in the refrigerator for about one month.

TO SERVE

Cool before using. Can be stored in a sealed jar or container in the refrigerator for about one month. To warm, place in a cup of warm water before serving.

VARIATIONS

May use any flavored Dark Balsamic Vinegar of your choice.

FAVORITE FRUITY DRESSING

Whole fruit fused Olive Oils, such as Blood Orange, Lime and Lemon, are so flavorful because the whole fruit and the olives are crushed together to make these exquisite oils. The tart-sweet flavor can't be beat.

Serves: 4–6

INGREDIENTS

¼ cup Premium White Balsamic Vinegar

3–4 tablespoons shallots, finely chopped

½ teaspoon Dijon mustard

½ teaspoon honey

3 tablespoons orange juice, either fresh squeezed or prepared

2 tablespoons fresh lemon juice

Salt and pepper to taste

METHOD

Place all ingredients in a large jar with a tight lid. Shake vigorously, making sure everything blends well.

TO SERVE

See Vinaigrette 101 for dressing the bowl method. Once dressed, serve right away.

VARIATIONS

🐟 This dressing stores well in the refrigerator for a few days. Bring to room temperature before using.

🐟 Try Lime or Lemon Olive Oil and consult the Pairings Section for a variety of White and Dark Balsamic Vinegar suggestions.

ZESTY GREEN DRIZZLE

Drizzles are a great way to enliven a dish and add color. This drizzle can be used over veggies to add more green power or in a salad. It is also delicious on prepared meat, chicken and fish or as a marinade. Select bunches of fresh herbs at the Farmer's Market, or start a little herb garden of your own either in large pots or in a small section of your backyard.

Makes about ½ cup

INGREDIENTS

1 cup fresh flat leaf parsley leaves, washed with stems, plus extra for garnish

½ cup fresh mint leaves, plus extra for garnish

2 tablespoons fresh lemon juice

1 teaspoon honey

¼ teaspoon salt

¼ cup Basil Olive Oil

1–2 tablespoons water, if needed to thin

METHOD

Using a food processor, pulse parsley, mint, lemon juice, and honey. Add salt and slowly add Basil Olive Oil. If needed, add a little water to thin. Pulse until smooth.

TO SERVE

Drizzles are typically applied to the plate before adding the food, or onto the top of the food. Either option makes a pleasing presentation.

VARIATIONS

🌿 You can substitute most any green, fresh vegetable or herb. Try fresh kale, spinach, Swiss chard, basil, cilantro, tarragon, sage or dill.

🐚 For an Asian flare, use Cilantro and Roasted Onion Olive Oil or Roasted Sesame Oil. Try flavored Olive Oils such as Garlic, Dill, Tarragon, or Mushroom and Sage. A few drops of Roasted Walnut will add a delicious, nutty flavor.

ALL THE DRIZZLE YOU'LL EVER NEED

Is it a drizzle or a sauce? No matter what you call it, these warm, luscious drizzles will dress up any plate while adding additional flavor. Add fresh ingredients, such as onions, scallions, garlic, shallots, leeks and/or chives for a distinctive aroma and healthy boost.

Makes ½ cup

INGREDIENTS

4 tablespoons Butter Olive Oil

1 tablespoon onion, garlic, shallot or scallion, finely chopped

2 tablespoons Traditional Dark or Premium White Balsamic Vinegar

2 tablespoons water

Salt and pepper to taste

METHOD

Sauté onion, garlic, shallot or scallion in Butter Olive Oil over medium heat for about 1–2 minutes. Add Balsamic Vinegar, salt and pepper. Heat for another 1–2 minutes.

TO SERVE

Drizzle on plate and place desired entrée on top or use as a topping.

Make this recipe spicy or herb-filled. If you use fresh ingredients, it will have a distinctive aroma and a healthy boost.

VARIATIONS

🌶️ This recipe can be made into a spicy or an herb-filled drizzle. For a hot flavor, try Chipotle, Harissa, or Green Chili Olive Oil. Milder options are Garlic, Basil, Herbes de Provence, Lemon, Lime, Mushroom and Sage, Rosemary or Dill Olive Oil.

🥄 Use a flavored Dark or White Balsamic Vinegar, referring to the Pairings Section in Part Three for the appropriate combination.

🌿 Try other herbs, such as lemongrass, chives, cilantro, mint, basil, rosemary, tarragon, sage, or oregano. Add spices such as cumin, chili powder, coriander, cayenne, or red pepper flakes.

BALSAMIC VINEGAR REDUCTION 101

Reductions and syrups add exquisite flavor to any dish. This reduction is great on salads, and as a sauce for vegetables, meat, fish, and chicken. Reductions add a gourmet flavor twist on desserts such as ice cream, fruit, cakes and berries.

Makes ¾ cup

INGREDIENTS

1 cup Traditional Dark Balsamic Vinegar

Always use a non-reactive saucepan, such as stainless steel, when making a reduction.

METHOD

Place Traditional Dark Balsamic Vinegar in a small non-reactive saucepan over medium heat and bring to a boil. Reduce heat to low, stirring frequently and let simmer for about 10 minutes or until vinegar has reduced down. Watch carefully as it can burn easily. When the vinegar coats the back of a spoon, you'll know it is ready.

Remove from heat and let cool. If refrigerated, it may harden but can be a placed in a bowl of warm water to soften.

Keeps up to one month in a sealed container in the refrigerator.

TO SERVE

Drizzle or spoon over your entrée, side or dessert.

VARIATIONS

- Use any flavored Dark Balsamic Vinegar of your choice.

- Additionally, you can add a cinnamon stick, orange rind, whole peppercorns, garlic cloves, or a sprig of herbs, such as rosemary, thyme, oregano, basil, and bay leaf.

SALADS

SKINNY GIRL
POTATO SALAD   24

30   MIGHTY MINT AND
ARUGULA SALAD

34

QUICK AS A
FLASH TOSSED
SALAD

28

NOT YOUR
GRANDMA'S
BEET SALAD

SAVORY PANGO MANGO
SALAD

27

32

CRUNCHY CARROT
SLAW

SKINNY GIRL POTATO SALAD

This is a light version of the usual mayonnaise-based potato salad. Using a medium to robust Extra-virgin Olive Oil and Premium White Balsamic Vinegar enhances the flavors in the other ingredients.

Serves: 6

INGREDIENTS

2 pounds potatoes, small red or Yukon gold, cut into ¾-inch cubes

4 cloves garlic, finely chopped

1 cup celery, diced

½ cup red onion, sliced

¼ cup fresh flat-leaf parsley, chopped

3 tablespoons Extra-virgin Olive Oil

1 tablespoon White Balsamic Vinegar

Salt and pepper, to taste

METHOD

Place potatoes in a large pot and cover with cold water. Lightly salt the water with about 1 teaspoon salt. Bring to boil, then reduce to simmer. After about 5 minutes, check the potatoes. You want the potatoes to be tender but to still hold their shape. May take 10–20 minutes, depending on size.

Drain and cool the potatoes, then peel and cut into bite-size chunks. Place potatoes, garlic, celery, onion and parsley in a large bowl and stir gently.

In a small bowl, combine Extra-virgin Olive Oil and White Balsamic Vinegar and whisk. Add to the other ingredients and mix well. Add salt and pepper to taste.

TO SERVE

Can be served at room temperature. If made in advance, refrigerate. Place in an attractive bowl and enjoy.

VARIATIONS

🌶 Most any flavored Olive Oil will work in this salad, including the whole-fruit fused oils. Flavored Dark Balsamic Vinegars will enhance the taste. See Pairings Section in Part Three for more options.

VARIATIONS

🫒 Blood Orange, Lemon, Cilantro and Roasted Onion, Basil, Garlic or Green Chili Olive Oil can be used. Try Honey Ginger, Lemongrass Mint, Oregano, Cranberry Pear, Peach or Tangerine Balsamic Vinegar.

SAVORY PANGO MANGO SALAD

Lighten up a heavy meal by serving this fruit salad as a side, or serve for lunch or as a snack. This salad is perfect when fresh tomatoes are available. At other times try blueberries, grapes, raspberries, peaches, nectarines, or plums.

Serves: 6

INGREDIENTS

¼ cup red onion, chopped

4 medium tomatoes, quartered or sliced

1 mango, peeled and diced

1 avocado, peeled and diced

2 tablespoons Jalapeño Balsamic Vinegar

5 tablespoons Lime Olive Oil

2 teaspoons fresh lime juice, plus lime slices for garnish

½ cup fresh cilantro, chopped, plus extra for garnish

Salt to taste

METHOD

In a large bowl, combine onion, tomatoes, mango, avocado, lime juice and mix gently. Add Jalapeño Balsamic Vinegar, Lime Olive Oil and salt and mix thoroughly. Refrigerate for about 20 minutes to give flavors time to blend.

TO SERVE

Remove from refrigerator. Add fresh cilantro and mix. Place in colorful bowl. Garnish with lime slices and cilantro sprigs.

NOT YOUR GRANDMA'S BEET SALAD

Beets and spinach are family. Combine them with crumbly goat cheese and voilá; a festive, tasty dish is yours. Grandma may have said to "eat your vegetables," but she never dreamed they could be this good.

Serves: 6

INGREDIENTS

8 medium-size beets, scrubbed, tops removed

Beet greens, washed, dried, chopped

2 cups baby spinach, washed and dried

½ cup + 3 tablespoons Lemon Olive Oil

¼ cup Tangerine Balsamic Vinegar

8 ounces goat cheese, crumbled

Salt and pepper to taste

Beets come in other colors besides the familiar red.

Try yellow or gold, or mix them up and use all three.

METHOD

Preheat oven to 400°. Combine whole beets with 3 tablespoons Lemon Olive Oil, place on baking pan and roast 40–60 minutes or until fork tender. Allow to cool and cut into small chunks.

In a large bowl place chopped beets, chopped beet greens and baby spinach.

Combine remainder of Lemon Olive Oil and Tangerine Balsamic Vinegar in a small bowl or jar with secure screw top. Whisk or shake vigorously. Gently pour the dressing over the beets and spinach, add salt and pepper and lightly toss.

TO SERVE

Place on individual salad plates and top with crumbled goat cheese. Serve.

VARIATIONS

- You can mix in other greens, such as arugula for a peppery taste, or use feta in place of goat cheese.

- Change up the Olive Oil and Vinegar pairing, and a whole new flavor is created.

- Try Tarragon Olive Oil and Cranberry Pear Balsamic Vinegar or Garlic Olive Oil and Neapolitan Herb Balsamic Vinegar.

MIGHTY MINT AND ARUGULA SALAD

The ancients believed that mint was a symbol of hospitality and wisdom. Its distinctive bouquet and flavor create a cool, refreshing sensation. Combining it with peppery arugula and sweet dates, salty cheese and the tangy sharp notes of nuts satisfies all the flavor cravings.

Serves: 4

INGREDIENTS

¼ cup fresh mint leaves

¼ cup fresh flat-leaf parsley leaves, stems removed

4 cups baby arugula

½ cup nuts – pecans, walnuts or almonds, toasted

¼ cup dates, chopped

4 ounces cheese, shaved – Parmigiano-Reggiano, Manchego, or Pecorino

METHOD

In a large bowl, toss mint, parsley, and arugula. Add nuts, dates and all the cheese except a few tablespoons to top the individual plates. Gently add Favorite Fruity Dressing – see page 17. Mix gently.

TO SERVE

Place on individual salad plates, top with remaining cheese and serve.

Fresh arugula is so tasty, and if you can get wild, organic arugula at your local Farmer's Market don't pass it up.

Mint takes to so many different soils and is so easy to grow, you'll have to contain it or it will take over the garden.

VARIATIONS

🌱 Try substituting spinach for the arugula.

🥗 Vinaigrette 101 can also be used to dress this salad. Or try one of these pairings, such as Cilantro and Roasted Onion and Lemongrass Mint Balsamic Vinegar, Lime Olive Oil and Cranberry Pear Balsamic Vinegar, or Dill Olive Oil and Honey Ginger Balsamic Vinegar, or Lemon Olive Oil and Neapolitan Herb Balsamic Vinegar to name just a few.

🌿 If you're an herb lover, add your favorite herbs such as tarragon, basil, thyme, oregano, chives, marjoram, cilantro, dill, chives and/or lemongrass.

CRUNCHY CARROT SLAW

Is it a slaw or a salad? This colorful side will enliven your palate as well as your table. Carrots are the superheroes of root vegetables and come in a variety of colors other than the popular orange color. Look for purple, red, white and yellow carrots the next time you visit the Farmer's Market. Raisins come in a variety of colors too. Check out black, green, blue, purple or yellow ones.

Serves: 4–6

INGREDIENTS

8 carrots, peeled or unpeeled, grated

½ cup walnuts or pecans, chopped and toasted

½ cup raisins

4 tablespoons Blood Orange Olive Oil

2 tablespoons fresh lemon juice

Salt to taste

METHOD

Using the large holes on a grater, grate carrots and place in a medium size bowl. Add chopped nuts and raisins. Drizzle with Blood Orange Olive Oil and lemon juice and mix gently and thoroughly. Add salt to taste.

Look for purple, red, white and yellow carrots the next time you visit the Farmer's Market.

TO SERVE

Place in serving bowl and serve as a side or a salad.

VARIATIONS

🫒 Use Lime or Lemon Olive Oil for another fruity alternative. Try Basil, Rosemary, or Herbes de Provence Olive Oil for an herbaceous flavor. Spice and heat it up with Harissa Olive Oil.

🖌 Replace the carrots with parsnips for a spicier flavor option.

QUICK AS A FLASH SALAD

The old stand-by just got upgraded. Enjoy a tossed salad with any meal. Dress it up or dress it down – it will be just right. And, no matter the season, there are always some type of greens that can be included in this simple, yet scrumptious salad.

Serves: 4–6

INGREDIENTS

6 cups lettuce, torn or whole – washed and drained. Can be mixed greens, such as butter lettuce, romaine, iceberg, frisee, radicchio, dandelion, chicory, romaine, arugula and/or escarole

12 cherry or grape tomatoes, cut in half

½ red onion, sliced

1 avocado, cubed

Salt and pepper to taste

METHOD

In a large bowl, place lettuce leaves, tomatoes, red onion, and avocado and mix gently.

TO SERVE

When ready to serve, dress bowl as described on page 15 in Dressings, Drizzles and Reductions. Then add salad and toss to mix. Serve right away.

VARIATIONS

🥄 Add other favorite ingredients, such as chopped fresh herbs, celery, carrots, radishes, toasted nuts, and/or fresh or dried fruit.

🧴 Dress with Favorite Fruity Dressing, page 17, or Vinaigrette 101, page 14.

🫙 Refer to Pairings Section in Part Three for more Olive Oil and Balsamic Vinegar combinations.

PASTA

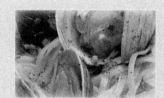

LIGHT LINGUIINI
AND CLAMS
36

EASY ANGEL HAIR WITH
BASIL PESTO
46

SIMPLE SHRIMP
AND SPINACH
FETTUCCINE

38

42
POTLUCK
PASTA
SALAD

40

OLD SCHOOL
BOLOGNESE

PERFECT PASTA
PRIMAVERA

44

LIGHT LINGUINI AND CLAMS

Whether you use fresh clams or canned, this favorite Mediterranean dish takes a few minutes to prepare and is sure to look and taste as if you've been cooking all day. Use plenty of fresh parsley for color and flavor. And even Venus, rising from her clamshell, could not have imagined how delicious this classic dish could be using flavored Olive Oil.

Serves: 4

INGREDIENTS

1 pound fresh clams or 3 cans clams, chopped, 6.5-ounce cans

1 bottle clam juice, 8 ounces

⅓ cup Basil Olive Oil

3 large cloves garlic, peeled and minced

Salt and pepper to taste

1 teaspoon dried red pepper flakes, or more to taste

⅓ cup basil, chopped, plus a few sprigs for garnish

½ cup flat-leaf parsley, stems removed and chopped, plus a few sprigs for garnish

1 pound linguini, cooked al dente

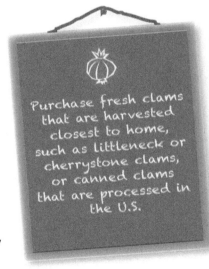

Purchase fresh clams that are harvested closest to home, such as Littleneck or cherrystone clams, or canned clams that are processed in the U.S.

METHOD

If using fresh clams, scrub and rinse in cold water, making sure each clam is closed. If any are open, discard.

In a large bowl, place clean clams in cold water and set aside for 30 minutes, then drain. In a large saucepan, heat Basil Olive Oil over low heat. Add garlic and sauté lightly. Add salt, pepper, red pepper flakes, basil and clam juice. Heat to simmer, then add fresh clams or canned clams. Cover and simmer about 2 minutes or until the clams open. If using canned clams, simmer clams until they are thoroughly heated.

Meanwhile, cook linguini al dente, according to package directions. Once cooked, drain, reserving ¼ cup pasta water. Place linguini in large bowl and mix in several tablespoons of the pasta water until all the pasta is coated. Then stir in clam broth and mix.

TO SERVE

Divide pasta into individual bowls, add clams to pasta, carefully lifting each clam if using fresh clams. Top with parsley and garnish. Serve immediately.

VARIATIONS

🌿 Tarragon, Herbes de Provence, Rosemary, Lemon or Lime Olive Oil turn this classic dish into your own one-of-a-kind.

SIMPLE SHRIMP AND SPINACH FETTUCCINE

Paired with a tossed salad, this recipe is sophisticated enough for a dinner party and simple enough to serve to the family on a week night. Cooking shrimp in butter is traditional, but using Butter Olive Oil instead of butter makes this dish new, light and fresh.

Serves: 4

INGREDIENTS

1 pound fettuccine

⅓ cup Butter Olive Oil, plus 2 tablespoons to drizzle

2 cloves garlic, sliced thin

1 pound medium shrimp, peeled and deveined

¼ teaspoon salt

¼ teaspoon pepper

1 bag fresh baby spinach, 6–7 ounces

¼ cup Parmesan cheese, shaved

1 tablespoon fresh rosemary leaves, plus extra sprigs for garnish

METHOD

Cook pasta al dente according to package directions.

In a large skillet, heat Butter Olive Oil over medium heat. Add garlic and sauté for less than a minute. Remove garlic and set aside. Increase heat to medium-high and add shrimp, salt and pepper and stir. Cook until shrimp are done—about 4–5 minutes or until opaque and slightly pink. Add pasta, spinach and garlic to shrimp and stir gently until spinach wilts.

TO SERVE

Remove from skillet and place in a large serving bowl. Drizzle Butter Olive Oil on top, then add cheese and rosemary. Garnish with rosemary sprigs.

VARIATIONS

☼ Rosemary Olive Oil can be used in combination with Butter Olive Oil or in place of it. Or try Dill, Garlic, Basil, Tarragon, Lemon, Lime, Tuscan Herb or Mushroom and Sage Olive Oil.

🥬 Instead of spinach, use arugula, Swiss chard, asparagus, broccoli or broccoli rabe. Add ½ cup fresh basil leaves with the spinach.

🍝 Other pastas that work well with this dish are penne, farfalle, linguini or spaghetti.

OLD SCHOOL BOLOGNESE SAUCE

This thick, rich and meaty sauce definitely qualifies as Old School. No matter the time of the year, Bolognese sauce is always a pleaser. Using flavored Olive Oil and Balsamic Vinegar adds an intensity that is irresistible.

Serves: 4

INGREDIENTS

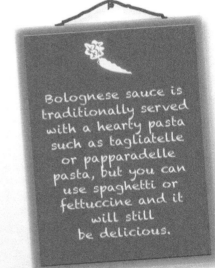

Bolognese sauce is traditionally served with a hearty pasta such as tagliatelle or papparadelle pasta, but you can use spaghetti or fettuccine and it will still be delicious.

¼ cup Tuscan Herb Olive Oil

3 garlic cloves, minced

⅔ cup onion, finely chopped

½ cup carrot, peeled and finely chopped

½ cup celery, finely chopped

1 pound ground beef, chuck or round

1 tablespoon Neapolitan Herb Balsamic Vinegar

1 can crushed tomatoes – 28-ounce can

¼ fresh flat-leaf parsley, chopped

⅓ cup fresh basil leaves, chopped, plus extra leaves for garnish

Salt and pepper to taste

¼ cup Parmesan or Romano Pecorino cheese, grated, plus a little extra for sprinkling

1 pound papparedelle pasta

METHOD

Heat Tuscan Herb Olive Oil in an extra-large skillet with a lid over a medium heat. Add garlic and onions and sauté a few minutes, making sure that garlic does not brown. Add carrots and celery and sauté for about 5 minutes. Increase the heat to high and add ground beef, stirring constantly and breaking up the lumps. Drizzle Neapolitan Herb Balsamic Vinegar over the meat and mix well.

When the meat is browned, lower the heat and add tomatoes, parsley, basil, salt and pepper. Cover and simmer sauce until it becomes thickened – about 30–40 minutes. Add cheese and stir. Salt and pepper to taste.

Cook pappardelle or your choice of pasta al dente according to package directions. Drain.

TO SERVE

Place pasta in large serving bowl. Take a ladle full of sauce and place over pasta, mixing gently until the pasta is lightly coated. Ladle over the remaining sauce, sprinkle a little cheese over the top, and garnish with whole basil leaves. Serve immediately.

VARIATIONS

- ☙ Pair Garlic Olive Oil and Champagne Balsamic Vinegar or Basil Olive Oil and Oregano Balsamic Vinegar or Mushroom and Sage Olive Oil and Fig Balsamic Vinegar and re-invent this traditional dish.

POTLUCK PASTA SALAD

Always the perfect side or an easy potluck dish, this salad has a fresh, spicy flavor. Cool it down or spice it up, depending on the choice of olive oil used.

Serves: 4

INGREDIENTS

1 pound pasta – preferably farfalle

1 red bell pepper, chopped

½ cup carrots, chopped

¼ cup red onion, chopped

1 cup black olives, halved

⅓ cup fresh mint, chopped, plus extra for garnish

½ cup Harissa Olive Oil

Extra-virgin Olive Oil, a drizzle

⅓ cup fresh basil, chopped, plus extra for garnish

3 cups fresh baby spinach, chopped

¼ cup Parmesan cheese

Salt to taste

Use fresh herbs and greens from the Farmer's Market or from your own garden.

METHOD

Cook pasta according to package directions. Drain and set aside to cool.

In a large serving bowl, combine cooled pasta and all ingredients except cheese. Mix well. Add Parmesan cheese and mix again. Add salt if needed. If dry, drizzle with Extra-virgin Olive Oil or additional Harissa Olive Oil.

TO SERVE

Garnish with basil and mint leaves.

VARIATIONS

🖐 You can use just about any type of small-size pasta for this salad, such as fusilli, elbows or penne.

✎ To turn down the heat, but still experience a little kick, use Chipotle Olive Oil.

🕯 Extra-virgin Olive Oil, Basil, Cilantro and Roasted Onion, Garlic, Herbes de Provence, Tarragon, Dill, or Tuscan Herb Olive Oil work well with this dish.

🌿 For an assortment of greens, add arugula or kale instead of spinach.

PERFECT PASTA PRIMAVERA

When fresh vegetables are plentiful and you're looking for ways to cook them, this dish is perfect! Why cover up the flavor of fresh vegetables with a heavy cream sauce? Try a lighter version of this favorite and save the cream for another time.

You can use as many of the vegetables listed below or as few as desired. Try adding asparagus, green peas, mushrooms or any of your favorites.

Serves: 4–6

INGREDIENTS

1 pound penne

¼ cup Herbes de Provence Olive Oil

3 tablespoons Lemon Olive Oil

1 zucchini, cut into rounds and quartered

1 yellow squash, cut into rounds and quartered

1 carrot, peeled and chopped

½ red bell pepper, chopped

½ pound sugar snap peas cut in half

½ cup small broccoli floret

2 cloves garlic, peeled and minced

1 pint cherry or grape tomatoes, halved

½ cup goat cheese, crumbled

⅓ cup fresh basil chopped

⅓ cup fresh parsley, chopped

½ cup Parmesan cheese

METHOD

In a large skillet, heat Herbes de Provence Olive Oil and Lemon Olive Oil over a medium heat. Add all ingredients except tomatoes, basil, parsley, Parmesan and goat cheese. Mix and sauté about 2 minutes – just long enough to heat the vegetables and coat them with Olive Oils. You want them crunchy, but not raw.

Cook pasta al dente according to package directions. Drain and add to the sautéed vegetables. Mix gently and add tomatoes, basil, parsley, Parmesan cheese and goat cheese. Salt and pepper to taste. Stir and mix gently.

TO SERVE

Place in serving bowl and serve immediately.

VARIATIONS

🍲 Use farfalle, fusilli, spaghetti, fettuccini or the pasta of your choice.

🍄 Try Garlic, Basil, Dill, Mushroom and Sage, Tuscan Herb, or Rosemary Olive Oil.

EASY ANGEL HAIR WITH BASIL PESTO

Wonder why pesto never goes out of style? It's because it's so tasty, versatile and good for you. Pesto is quick to make, uses garden fresh ingredients, and gives entrées, salads and appetizers a seasonal flavor. Pesto is great on grilled bread, or used as a topping on fish, vegetables, eggs or added to soups or salads for an extra dash of flavor.

Here is a classic pesto using fresh basil and Extra-virgin Olive Oil. See Variations below for ingredients that can be used to make your own signature pesto.

Serves: 4–6

> Pesto stores well in an airtight container in the refrigerator for up to 2 days. Place pesto in the container, then cover the top with a thin layer of Extra-virgin Olive Oil. This will help keep its fresh, green color.

INGREDIENTS

2 cups fresh basil leaves, packed – approximately 2 bunches with extra leaves for garnish

1 large garlic clove, peeled

½ cup Extra-virgin Olive Oil – robust

¼ cup pine nuts

½ cup Parmigiano-Reggiano cheese, grated

Salt and pepper to taste

1 pound angel hair, cooked al dente

METHOD

Combine basil, garlic, pine nuts and olive oil in a blender or food processor. Pulse to a purée. Add cheese, salt and pepper, then pulse again. Taste, making sure there is enough salt and pepper. Place pesto in serving bowl.

Cook angel hair al dente according to package directions. Drain and transfer to serving bowl and mix gently, coating the pasta with the pesto.

TO SERVE

Drizzle with olive oil, garnish with basil leaves and serve immediately.

VARIATIONS

🌿 Instead of fresh basil leaves, use fresh parsley, cilantro, mint, thyme, arugula, spinach, kale, or broccoli rabe, depending on the season.

🥜 Instead of pine nuts, try walnuts, cashews, almonds, sunflower or pumpkin seeds.

🖊 Flavored olive oils complement this dish very well. Try Garlic, Basil, Herbes de Provence, Lemon, Tuscan Herb, Butter, Rosemary or Dill Olive Oil.

🍝 Try other types of pastas such as spaghetti, capellini, fusilli, or farfalle.

🖊 Adding 2 tablespoons flax, hemp or chia seeds to the blender increases the health benefit and nutty flavor.

POTATOES, RICE & GRAINS

58

HEARTY QUINOA
TABOULEH

56

TANGY
TOASTED
COUSCOUS

TWICE AS
NICE RICE

54

EASY PEASY HERB RISOTTO

48

POTATOES
MANCHESTER

50

52

BETTER THAN
FRIED SWEET
POTATO FRIES

EASY PEASY HERB RISOTTO

Green peas are such a tasty addition to most any dish. They add color and texture and, of course, a lot of flavor. If fresh peas are not available, frozen peas work just as well. You can add other vegetables to this risotto recipe, along with different flavored olive oils, to make it your own. Risotto can be prepared with chicken or vegetable stock. It should be cooked al dente, with a soft outer coating and a firm inner one, creating a creamy or slightly soupy consistency.

Serves: 4

INGREDIENTS

7 cups chicken or vegetable stock

⅔ cup onion, chopped

2 cloves garlic, minced

¼ cup Mushroom and Sage Olive Oil

1½ cups Arborio rice

½ cup Sicilian Lemon White Balsamic Vinegar

2 cups fresh herbs, chopped – parsley, tarragon, chives, dill, basil, plus extra for garnish

Handful fresh spinach and/or arugula – optional

1 cup green peas

½ cup Romano cheese, grated

Salt and pepper to taste

METHOD

In a saucepan, simmer stock. In a medium bowl, place chopped herbs and optional greens and set aside.

In a large skillet, heat Mushroom and Sage Olive Oil and sauté onion and garlic until soft – about 3 minutes. Stir in rice and coat with mixture. Add Sicilian Lemon Balsamic Vinegar and stir until it is absorbed.

Begin adding stock about ½ cup at a time. It should just cover the rice. Cook slowly, stirring continually – about 20 minutes. Taste and if still very hard, add a little more stock and stir. Simmer a few more minutes. When done, stir in herbs, peas, cheese, salt and pepper.

TO SERVE

Place in warm shallow bowls or on preheated plates. Serve immediately.

VARIATIONS

🍶 Herbes de Provence, Basil, Tarragon, Lemon, Lime, Rosemary or Tuscan Herb Olive Oil will add additional flavor to this dish. Pair any of these Olive Oils with Sicilian Lemon or Neapolitan Herb Balsamic Vinegar. Consult the Pairings Section, Part Three, for other flavorful combinations.

POTATOES MANCHESTER

Making roasted potatoes is quick and easy, especially using this recipe.
Experiment with different flavored Olive Oils and you have a new dish every time.

Serves: 4–6

INGREDIENTS

6 medium Yukon potatoes – about 2 pounds, peeled and cut into chunks
1-inch thick

4 tablespoons Extra-virgin Olive Oil, plus a little extra for drizzling

Salt and pepper to taste

METHOD

Preheat oven to 425°. Peel, cut and rinse potatoes.
In a large pot, place potatoes and a pinch of
salt in water. Boil for about 5 minutes. Strain in a
colander.

Place potatoes in a large baking dish and
thoroughly coat with olive oil, salt and pepper.
After coating, be sure there is space between each
potato so that the sides are exposed to the hot air
of the oven. This will help them to brown nicely.
Roast for about 20 minutes, then turn. Roast an
additional 20 minutes or until brown.

More than 100
varieties of potatoes
are grown in the
United States,
including russets,
red, white, yellow,
purple, fingerlings
and petites, to
mention a few.

Check out your local
Farmer's Market
to find out which
types of potatoes are
grown close to you.

TO SERVE

Place in serving bowl and serve while nice and hot.
Drizzle with additional olive oil, if desired.

VARIATIONS

🌣 Most any flavored Olive Oil will complement potatoes. Try Basil, Butter, Garlic, Herbes de Provence, Tarragon, Tuscan Herb, Rosemary, or Mushroom and Sage Olive Oil. For potatoes with spice, Harissa, Green Chili or Chipotle Olive Oil will add heat.

BETTER THAN FRIED SWEET POTATO FRIES

Packed with nutrition and a sweet flavor, sweet potatoes are low on the glycemic index scale and loaded with vitamins, antioxidants and fiber. Look for the colorful varieties available at the Farmer's Market, such as orange, orange-red, white and purple. Eat them with the skins on for more health benefits and a prettier presentation. Here's a recipe that proves you can have your fries and eat them too.

Serves: 4

INGREDIENTS

2 medium sweet potatoes, cut into spears with skin on

3–4 tablespoons Garlic Olive Oil

2 tablespoons Maple Balsamic Vinegar

Salt and pepper to taste

METHOD

Pre-heat oven to 450°. Cut potatoes into spears. Place on a baking sheet and sprinkle with Garlic Olive Oil, Maple Balsamic Vinegar, salt and pepper. Mix thoroughly. Spread evenly and bake for about 15 minutes. Mix again thoroughly, turning potatoes and bake an additional 5–10 minutes or until lightly browned.

TO SERVE

Place on serving platter. Sprinkle with salt. Serve immediately.

VARIATIONS

- Try Chipotle Olive Oil and Cinnamon Pear Balsamic Vinegar, robust Extra-virgin Olive Oil and Traditional Dark Balsamic Vinegar, Blood Orange Olive Oil and Maple Balsamic Vinegar, or Garlic Olive Oil and Neapolitan Herb Balsamic Vinegar.

White-fleshed sweet potatoes make this an extra-flavorful dish.

TWICE AS NICE RICE

This dish is a take on the many variations of chickpeas and rice made in the Middle East. It's versatile because you can substitute other legumes such as lentils for the chickpeas and brown or wild rice for the white rice. The citrusy notes add flavor and complement the crunchiness of the nuts and rice. The fresh herbs add light flavor.

Serves: 4–6

INGREDIENTS

2 tablespoons Blood Orange Olive Oil

½ onion, chopped

1 cup long grain rice, uncooked

2 cups vegetable or chicken broth

½ cup orange juice

½ cup dried cherries

1 can chickpeas, 15 ounces, drained and rinsed

½ cup sliced almonds, toasted

¼ cup fresh flat-leaf parsley, chopped, stems removed, plus extra for garnish

¼ cup fresh mint leaves, chopped, plus extra for garnish

Salt and pepper to taste

Although rice from all over the world is available, look for the many varieties that are grown in the United States too. They are easily found in the grocery store and at the Farmer's Market.

METHOD

In a large skillet, heat Blood Orange Olive Oil over medium-high heat. Sauté onions, cooking until softened – about 5 minutes. Add rice and coat thoroughly with mixture. Add broth, orange juice and chickpeas and bring to a boil. Reduce heat, cover and simmer until rice is done — about 20–30 minutes.

Add cherries, almonds, herbs, salt and pepper. Gently fluff.

TO SERVE

Place rice in a serving bowl. Garnish with parsley and mint leaves. Serve immediately.

VARIATIONS

🍋 Lemon or Lime Olive Oil are great in this dish.

🍇 Try pine nuts or walnuts instead of almonds. Use dried currants, raisins, or craisins instead of cherries.

🌿 Other herbs that work well are fresh oregano or fresh cilantro.

TANGY TOASTED COUSCOUS

Couscous is a light and fluffy staple that is eaten throughout the world. Its popularity in the U.S. continues to grow. The beauty of couscous is that it picks up the flavor of whatever it is cooked with, and it is a perfect accompaniment to soups, stews, chicken and meats. Most any type of fresh vegetable can be combined with couscous, depending on the season.

Serves: 4–6

INGREDIENTS

1½ cups couscous

3 cups water

5 tablespoons Lemon Olive Oil

12 asparagus spears, cut into 1 inch pieces

1 yellow squash, cut into 1 inch pieces

1 red bell pepper, seeded and sliced

1 yellow bell pepper, seeded and sliced

3 tablespoons Apricot Balsamic Vinegar

1 tablespoon fresh oregano leaves, chopped, plus extra for garnish

1 tablespoon fresh thyme leaves, chopped, plus extra for garnish

Salt and pepper to taste

METHOD

Preheat oven 450°. In a large baking dish, combine vegetables and 3 tablespoons Lemon Olive Oil, salt and pepper. Mix gently. Roast for 10–12 minutes or until just tender. Remove from oven and mix in herbs.

In a saucepan, add 2 tablespoons Lemon Olive Oil over medium heat. Add couscous, mix thoroughly and toast until lightly brown, stirring constantly, about 3–5 minutes. Add water and bring to a boil. Lower heat, cover and simmer for about 10–12 minutes.

TO SERVE

In a large serving bowl, combine couscous, vegetables and Apricot Balsamic Vinegar and toss. Add salt and pepper if needed. Garnish with oregano and thyme leaves and serve.

VARIATIONS

✎ Traditional Dark Balsamic Vinegar will give this a rich flavor. Other flavored Balsamic Vinegars, such as Pomegranate, Dark Cherry, Fig, Jalapeño, Oregano, Sicilian Lemon, Neapolitan Herb and Tangerine can also be used.

🫒 For Olive Oils, try Green Chili, Chipotle or Harissa for a kick. Lime, Blood Orange, Garlic, Basil, or Dill Olive Oils are also flavorful options.

HEARTY QUINOA TABOULEH

Quinoa went from mostly unknown to gaining a reputation as the super grain of the century! Here's a new twist on an old-world tabouleh recipe. Using quinoa instead of bulgur wheat raises the flavor, fiber and protein content of this ancient dish.

Serves: 4

INGREDIENTS

1 cup uncooked quinoa

1¾ cup water

1 cucumber, peeled or striped, and chopped

1 small tomato, chopped

¼ cup red onion, sliced

¼ cup fresh parsley, chopped, plus extra for garnish

½ cup fresh mint, chopped, plus extra for garnish

Juice of 1 lemon

¼ – ½ cup Lemon Olive Oil

Salt and pepper to taste

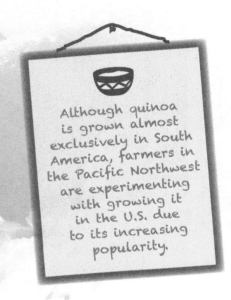

Although quinoa is grown almost exclusively in South America, farmers in the Pacific Northwest are experimenting with growing it in the U.S. due to its increasing popularity.

METHOD

Rinse quinoa and place quinoa and water in medium saucepan. Cover and simmer 20 minutes, or until liquid is absorbed. Remove from heat and place in medium size bowl.

Combine all ingredients, beginning with ¼ cup Lemon Olive Oil, and stir. Add more Lemon Olive Oil if dry. Cover and let stand about 1 hour.

TO SERVE

If not serving immediately, may refrigerate and serve chilled or at room temperature. Place in a serving bowl and garnish with fresh parsley and/or fresh mint.

VARIATIONS

- Try Lime or Blood Orange Olive Oil for additional options. Try Harissa, Green Chili or Chipotle Olive Oil for a spicier option. Dill or Rosemary Olive Oil will turn up the herbaceous flavor.

- Add canned chickpeas or black beans or fresh or frozen green peas for added protein and color.

MEATS

LIVELY LAMB
KABOBS   60

68
SAUCY
BALSAMIC
SLIDERS

NEW FAVORITE CHICKEN
70

64   FARM FRESH
          ROASTED
          CHICKEN

BALSAMIC
BEEF
TENDERLOIN
62

PEACHY PORK CHOPS

66

LIVELY LAMB KABOBS

Kabobs are the perfect meal for a big group. They can be broiled in the oven or on the grill outside. In just a few minutes, a tasty meal is yours. Use rosemary stems for skewers for added flavor (see Fancy Grilled Cherry Tomatoes for instructions) or use regular skewers.

Serves: 6–8

INGREDIENTS

1½ pounds leg of lamb or shoulder, trimmed and cut into ½-inch to 1-inch cubes

2 red bell peppers, cut into ½-inch to 1-inch cubes

2 red onions, peeled and quartered

5 tablespoons Harissa Olive Oil

2 tablespoons fresh rosemary leaves, plus extra sprigs for garnish

Salt and pepper to taste

METHOD

Heat the broiler or fire up the grill. In a large bowl, place trimmed and cut lamb, peppers, onions, Harissa Olive Oil, rosemary leaves, salt and pepper and mix thoroughly.

Using rosemary spikes or regular skewers, thread meat, bell peppers and onions, alternately. Place in broiler or on grill, turning regularly, for about 5 minutes. Meat should be slightly charred on the outside and pink on the inside.

TO SERVE

Place on serving platter. Garnish with rosemary sprigs and enjoy.

VARIATION

🌶 Chipotle or Green Chili Olive Oil are lively options. Rosemary, Garlic, and Tarragon Olive Oils are perfect for the milder palate.

Harissa Olive Oil is
the secret ingredient
here. It gives
the lamb a spicy,
smoky flavor.

BALSAMIC BEEF TENDERLOIN

This is the perfect go-to for guests or a family gathering. Beef tenderloin is one of the easiest meats to prepare. It tastes delicious and always makes a tempting presentation. With all the flavored Dark Balsamic Vinegars available, the options are endless.

Serves: 4–6

INGREDIENTS

1½ pounds beef tenderloin roast, trimmed and tied

2 tablespoons Mushroom and Sage Olive Oil

3 tablespoons Dijon mustard

3 tablespoons Fig Balsamic Vinegar

Coarse ground salt and coarsely cracked pepper

Check out your Farmer's Market for local growers of chemical-free, grass-fed livestock for increased flavor and health benefits. Most grocery stores now carry grass-fed beef.

METHOD

Preheat oven to 500°. Trim off the chain, silverskin and excess fat. Using butcher string, tie the tenderloin in 1½-inch to 2-inch intervals to keep its shape intact. Line a large baking pan with aluminum foil. Coat beef with Mushroom and Sage Olive Oil and place in pan.

In a small bowl, combine mustard, Fig Balsamic Vinegar and salt and mix thoroughly. Using a small brush, coat the meat with the mixture. Sprinkle pepper liberally over the meat.

Place in oven and roast for 25–28 minutes for medium-rare. For accuracy, use a meat thermometer and roast until it registers 125° for a medium-rare result.

Remove from oven and cover with aluminum foil. Let it rest in the pan for about 10–15 minutes before slicing.

TO SERVE

Place sliced tenderloin on serving platter and serve.

VARIATIONS

🌱 Coating the tenderloin with flavored Olive Oil and Balsamic Vinegar increases the taste. Try Chipotle Olive Oil and Dark Espresso Balsamic Vinegar, or Garlic Olive Oil and Pomegranate Balsamic Vinegar. Consult Pairings in Section Three and create your own sensational combination.

🌿 Check out Dressings, Drizzles and Reductions for a delicious accompaniment, such as Zesty Green Drizzle or Tangy Balsamic Syrup.

FARM FRESH ROASTED CHICKEN

A cooked, golden-brown whole hen is a beautiful sight. Make this dish for Sunday dinner or pep up the mid-week by surprising your family with this always-good favorite. The delicious taste of a locally raised, free-range hen will astound you. This one-dish meal is easy to prepare and in less than an hour you'll have a fabulous, healthy and attractive dinner on the table.

Serves: 4

INGREDIENTS

1 whole hen – 3 to 3½ pounds

1 small baby romaine – about 12–15 leaves

4 tablespoons Rosemary Olive Oil

½ cup lemon juice

6 cloves garlic, peeled

1 pound small potatoes, unpeeled

1 cup green peas, fresh or frozen – optional

3 tablespoons capers, rinsed and drained

Salt and pepper to taste

2–3 fresh rosemary sprigs for garnish

METHOD

Preheat oven to 450°. Rinse hen and dry well inside and outside with paper towels. Place hen in a large roasting pan. Rub with Rosemary Olive Oil, inside and out, then drizzle lemon juice all over. Sprinkle with salt and pepper. Add garlic and potatoes around the hen. Roast for 45 minutes, then add peas, romaine and capers. Continue to roast another 15 minutes until done.

TO SERVE

Place hen on serving platter. Surround with vegetables. Garnish with rosemary sprigs. Serve immediately.

VARIATIONS

Use Lemon, Lime, Butter, Tarragon, Tuscan Herb, or Mushroom and Sage Olive Oil.

Try fresh endive, radicchio or fennel instead of baby romaine.

PEACHY PORK CHOPS

When peaches are in season, it's pure happiness. Use ripe peaches and brush them with balsamic vinegar before cooking and you've got a treat. Combine them with pork for the ultimate duo. Keep an eye on these chops when grilling or baking. Overcooking will make them dry.

Serves: 4

INGREDIENTS

4 pork loin or end-loin chops, bone-in, 1-inch thick

3 tablespoons Mushroom and Sage Olive Oil

2 large peaches, ripe, quartered

2 tablespoons Maple Balsamic Vinegar

Salt and pepper to taste

⅓ cup fresh basil, chopped, plus sprigs for garnish

METHOD

Remove pork chops from refrigerator. Trim excess fat and let stand for about 30 minutes.

Brush pork chops with about 1 tablespoon Mushroom and Sage Olive Oil, salt and pepper. In a small bowl, combine peaches, Maple Balsamic Vinegar, the remainder of the Mushroom and Sage Olive Oil, and pepper. Toss and coat the peaches thoroughly. Set aside.

To Grill: Using a pre-heated grill pan or outdoor grill, place the pork chops on the grill and cook 3–4 minutes on each side or until firm and cooked. Place peaches on grill pan and sear, about 1 minute total, turning with tongs until peaches are golden.

To Bake: Preheat oven to 350°. Place pork chops in roasting pan and top with peaches. Bake for 20 minutes or until the chops are no longer pink.

TO SERVE

Place chops and peaches on serving platter. Drizzle the remaining Maple Balsamic Vinegar mixture over the top. Garnish with fresh basil. Serve immediately.

VARIATIONS

🍶 Try using Cinnamon Pear Balsamic Vinegar with Mushroom and Sage Olive Oil.

🏺 Or combine Garlic Olive Oil and Fig Balsamic for a tasty mix.

🍶 Butter Olive Oil and Maple Balsamic or Cinnamon Pear Balsamic work well with this dish too.

SAUCY BALSAMIC SLIDERS

Sliders are always sure to please. These mini-hamburgers are easy to make, serve and eat. Adults love them as much as kids do. And with the special ingredients of Dark Balsamic Vinegar and Extra-virgin Olive Oil, you'll have everyone wanting your recipe. Taking the extra step to brush the buns with flavored Olive Oil and toasting them makes a big impact.

Serves: Makes about 12 sliders

INGREDIENTS

2 pounds ground beef – 80% lean and 20% fat

4 tablespoons Chipotle Olive Oil, plus extra for buns

2 tablespoons Dark Chocolate Balsamic Vinegar

1 tablespoon Dijon mustard

3 cloves garlic, peeled and minced

Salt and pepper to taste

12 small buns or rolls

Condiments:

    6 ounces cheese, grated, such as Swiss, Gruyere or Jarlsberg

    3 small tomatoes, sliced

    1 small red onion, sliced

METHOD

In a large bowl, place ground meat. Add remaining ingredients and mix gently, combining well. Shape into 2-inch round patties, ½-inch thick. Pre-heat grill pan or outdoor grill. Place sliders on grill and cook for about 4 minutes, turning over and cooking an additional 4–5 minutes. If using cheese, add it to the sliders for the last 2 minutes of cooking time.

Slice buns and brush with Chipotle Olive Oil. Place cut side down on grill for the last 30 seconds. Or, place them on a baking sheet cut side up and broil for 30 seconds in the oven.

TO SERVE

Place on serving plate with condiments. Serve immediately.

VARIATIONS

🌶 Try Maple Balsamic Vinegar with Chipotle Olive Oil for a sweet-smoky combination.

🥄 Traditional Dark Balsamic Vinegar with Tarragon Olive Oil is very flavorful. So are Neapolitan Herb Balsamic Vinegar and Garlic Olive Oil. Green Chili Olive Oil and Dark Espresso Balsamic Vinegar really turns up the heat.

🦋 For Olive Oils, try Green Chili, Chipotle or Harissa for a kick. Lime, Blood Orange, Garlic, Basil or Dill Olive Oils are also flavorful options.

NEW FAVORITE CHICKEN

This chicken can be served with any of the drizzles or reductions in this book, but it is especially good with the Zesty Green Drizzle on page 18. You'll get your protein and a double dose of greens, especially using all these herbs. Cook this outside on the grill, use a grill pan on top of the stove, or bake in the oven.

Serves: 4

INGREDIENTS

4 chicken breast halves, boneless and skinless, approximately 8 ounces per breast

2 tablespoons Herbes de Provence Olive Oil

Juice and zest from 1 lemon

4 cloves garlic, peeled and chopped

3 tablespoons fresh flat-leaf parsley, chopped, plus sprigs for garnish

3 tablespoons fresh thyme, chopped, plus sprigs for garnish

2 tablespoons fresh rosemary, chopped, plus sprigs for garnish

¼ teaspoon salt

¼ teaspoon pepper

METHOD

Place chicken breasts in a medium size baking dish. Set aside. In a medium bowl, place all ingredients except chicken breasts and mix thoroughly. Spread mixture over each chicken breast. Cover and refrigerate for about 30 minutes. Heat outdoor grill or grill pan. Remove chicken from mixture and pat with paper towels to remove excess moisture.

To Grill: Grill until chicken feels firm to the touch and juices run clear, turning once.

To Bake: Bake at 350° for 20–30 minutes or until firm and juices run clear.

TO SERVE

If using a Drizzle, place a large spoonful of drizzle on the plate and top with a chicken breast. Garnish with fresh herbs. Drizzle can also be served on the side.

VARIATIONS

🐾 Just about any flavored olive will complement this chicken. Try Lemon, Lime, Mushroom and Sage, Rosemary, Dill, Basil, Butter, Tuscan Herb, Blood Orange Olive Oil. For a spicier option, try Green Chili or Chipotle Olive Oil.

SEAFOOD

 SIZZLING SHRIMP

74

TASTY TUNA 82

78
FISH TACOS ROCKAPULCO

EASIEST EVER SALMON 76

72

 HONEY GINGER SHRIMP

HEALTHY HALIBUT

80

HONEY GINGER SHRIMP

Give your shrimp from close-to-home-waters an Asian flair using fresh ginger and delicious Honey Ginger Balsamic Vinegar. You'll be supporting your health and the environment by eating seafood from waters as nearby as possible. Do the research and the taste test, and you will find that Atlantic wild shrimp and/or Gulf shrimp are fresher and taste so delicious.

Serves: 4

INGREDIENTS

1 pound medium shrimp, cleaned, deveined, with tails on

¼ cup Lemon Olive Oil, plus approximately 6 tablespoons for sauté

Juice of 1 lime, plus a few lime wedges for garnish

1 large clove garlic, cut in half

1 tablespoon fresh ginger, chopped

3 tablespoons Honey Ginger Balsamic Vinegar

⅓ cup fresh Thai Basil, plus a few sprigs for garnish

METHOD

Put all ingredients except shrimp in a food processor and pulse until just about smooth. In a plastic zip lock bag or a large bowl, place shrimp in the mixture, cover and marinate no more than 30 minutes.

Remove shrimp from marinade and set aside. Sauté shrimp in two batches so they are not overcrowded in the pan. Heat about 3 tablespoons of Lemon Olive Oil per batch over medium heat. Add shrimp and sauté. Once the shrimp just begin to turn pink, add enough marinade to allow them to finish cooking, while deglazing the pan with the marinade. Once shrimp are pink, remove. Repeat until all shrimp are cooked.

TO SERVE

Place shrimp in serving bowl. Garnish with basil sprigs and lime wedges. Serve immediately.

VARIATIONS

🍋 If fresh Thai Basil is not available, use Italian basil. Try Garlic, Basil, or Lime Olive Oil. Thai Lemongrass Mint Balsamic Vinegar will give this dish a fresh taste of mint.

SIZZLING SHRIMP

This shrimp has heat! So if that doesn't appeal to you, see Variations below to cut down the heat and still keep the flavor. It's an easy dish to serve for a large or small crowd, and can be combined with Twice As Nice Rice (page 54) for a one-dish meal. Up to 90% of the shrimp available come from Southeast Asia and many are farm-raised. Atlantic wild shrimp and Gulf shrimp are often available, and, for a few dollars more, you'll be getting a fresher and tastier product. For that reason, you'll eat less and savor more.

Serves: 4

INGREDIENTS

1 pound medium shrimp, peeled and deveined

5 tablespoons Harissa Olive Oil

2 tablespoons Coconut Balsamic Vinegar

3 cloves garlic, peeled and minced

2 tablespoons fresh lemon juice, plus lemon slices for garnish

3 tablespoons fresh flat leaf parsley, chopped, stems removed, plus extra for garnish

METHOD

In a large skillet, heat Harissa Olive Oil over medium heat. Add garlic and sauté for about 1 minute. Increase heat to high and add shrimp, Coconut Balsamic Vinegar, and lemon juice. Sauté until shrimp turn pink – about 2–3 minutes. Add salt and pepper to taste.

TO SERVE

Place in serving dish, top with parsley. Garnish with parsley sprigs and lemon slices. Serve immediately.

VARIATIONS

🍋 Try Lemon, Lime Olive Oil or Dill Olive Oil with Coconut Balsamic Vinegar. Or try Chipotle, Green Chili or Garlic Olive Oil with Sicilian Lemon Balsamic Vinegar.

🌿 Substitute fresh dill for the parsley.

EASIEST EVER SALMON

Baked, grilled or broiled, salmon's bold flavor always comes through. This recipe can be prepared in a matter of minutes and you'll have a healthy, protein-filled dinner on the table in no time.

Serves: 4

INGREDIENTS

4 salmon fillets, about 1-inch thick, 5–7 ounces

5 tablespoons Lemon Olive Oil

Salt and pepper to taste

3 tablespoons fresh basil, chopped, plus a few sprigs for garnish

METHOD

If using a grill pan, preheat pan. If baking, preheat oven to 400°. Coat salmon fillets with 2 tablespoons Lemon Olive Oil, salt and pepper. Place on grill pan skin-side down and cook 4–5 minutes each side, turning once. If baking, place in roasting pan with cover skin-side down and bake covered 12–15 minutes or until flaky.

TO SERVE

Place cooked fillets on serving platter. Drizzle with remaining Lemon Olive Oil. Top with chopped basil for garnish. Serve immediately.

VARIATIONS

🍲 Any of the whole fruit or whole herb fused olive oils work well with this fish. Try Lime Olive Oil, Blood Orange Olive Oil, Rosemary or Dill Olive Oil.

🍥 Substitute fresh dill for the basil.

Look for wild
salmon from the icy
cold waters of the
United States.

FISH TACOS ROCKAPULCO

Enjoy a summertime favorite, no matter what time of the year. Tacos are easy to put together and fun to serve—a perfect meal for a large group. These are so delicious and energizing, you just may want to pick up a surfboard and hang ten in the cool waters of Rockaway Beach!

Serves: 4

TACOS

INGREDIENTS

1 pound white fish such as cod, roughy, tilapia or hake, cut into large, bite-size chunks

⅓ cup flour

1 teaspoon chili powder

1 teaspoon ground cumin

1 teaspoon red pepper flakes

¼ teaspoon celery salt

Pinch of dried oregano

Pinch of black pepper

⅓ cup Extra-virgin Olive Oil

12 corn tortillas, heated

METHOD

In a medium bowl, combine flour and the spices. Stir and mix thoroughly. Coat each piece of fish with flour mixture. Set aside.

Heat olive oil in a large skillet to medium-high. Fry fish until brown on one side. Turn and continue to fry. Remove from skillet and set aside.

TACO SLAW

INGREDIENTS

¼ red cabbage, shredded

1 tablespoon red onion, finely chopped

2 tablespoons Coconut Balsamic Vinegar

3 teaspoons fresh cilantro, stems removed, chopped

1 tablespoon Green Chili Olive Oil

1 teaspoon fresh jalapeño, finely diced

1 teaspoon honey

Salt and pepper to taste

METHOD

In a large bowl, combine cabbage, onion, cilantro and jalapeño. Set aside. In a small bowl, whisk Green Chili Olive Oil, honey, salt and pepper. Pour into large bowl, dressing the cabbage combination. Set aside.

GUACAMOLE

INGREDIENTS

2 avocados, peeled, pit removed, cut into chunks

½ fresh jalapeño, finely diced

½ medium tomato, chopped

2 tablespoon fresh cilantro, stems removed, chopped

2 teaspoons red onion, finely chopped

Juice of ½ lime, plus lime slices to garnish

Pinch of cumin

Pinch of cayenne – optional

Salt and pepper to taste

METHOD

Combine all ingredients except tomatoes and mash to desired consistency. Add tomatoes and gently mix in. Set aside.

TORTILLAS

Preheat oven to 350°. On a large baking sheet, place tortillas and heat about 2–3 minutes or until warm.

TO SERVE

Place a tortilla on an individual plate. Add fish, guacamole and slaw. If adding hot sauce and sour cream, now is the time to place it on the tacos. Serve immediately.

CONDIMENTS – OPTIONAL

On each taco, add a dash of your favorite hot sauce, a dollop of sour cream, or fresh chopped cilantro.

VARIATIONS

🫒 Pineapple, Peach and Apricot Balsamic Vinegar add a fresh, fruity flavor. For additional kick, try Jalapeño Balsamic Vinegar.

HEALTHY HALIBUT

A lean, firm and flaky fish with a delicate flavor, halibut is worthy of your love. It has heart healthy fats and is so good for you.

Serves: 4

INGREDIENTS

4 halibut steaks, 5–7 ounces each

6 tablespoons Basil Olive Oil, plus a little extra to coat baking dish

2 tablespoons Tangerine Balsamic Vinegar

2 cloves garlic, peeled

1 cup fresh mint, chopped, plus extra for garnish

1–2 lemons, cut into slices

Salt and pepper to taste

METHOD

Preheat oven to 300°. Coat the bottom of a baking pan with Basil Olive Oil and layer lemon slices on the bottom of the pan. Sprinkle both sides of the steaks with salt and pepper and place in the pan. Bake about 8 minutes. The fish will appear opaque when done.

While fish is baking, combine Basil Olive Oil, Tangerine Balsamic Vinegar, garlic and fresh mint in blender or food processor. Pulse until smooth. Taste and add more salt and pepper if needed.

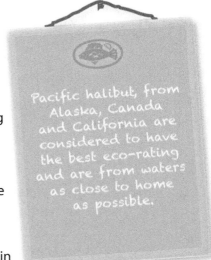

Pacific halibut, from Alaska, Canada and California are considered to have the best eco-rating and are from waters as close to home as possible.

TO SERVE

Place a large spoonful of sauce on individual plates and top with fish, mint and a lemon slice. Garnish with mint. Serve immediately.

VARIATIONS

🦐 For a savory taste, try Tarragon Olive Oil and Sicilian Lemon Balsamic Vinegar or Tuscan Herb Olive Oil and Oregano Balsamic Vinegar or Lime Olive Oil and Neapolitan Herb Balsamic Vinegar or Herbes de Provence Olive Oil and Pomegranate Balsamic Vinegar. See Part Three – Pairings for additional suggestions.

TASTY TUNA

Easy to prepare using oil-packed sundried tomatoes, this meal will come together quickly. Take care not to overcook tuna as it will dry out.

Serves: 4

INGREDIENTS

4 tuna fillets – about 6–7 ounces

5 tablespoons Dill Olive Oil, plus a drizzle to coat fillets

¼ cup olive oil packed sun-dried tomatoes, drained and chopped, reserving olive oil

1 clove garlic, peeled and minced

4 tablespoons fresh lemon juice

3 tablespoons oil from sun-dried tomatoes

¼ cup oil-cured black olives, chopped

½ cup fresh mint, chopped, plus extra for garnish

½ teaspoon orange zest, plus extra for garnish

Salt and pepper to taste

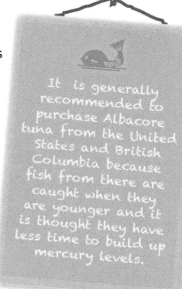

It is generally recommended to purchase Albacore tuna from the United States and British Columbia because fish from there are caught when they are younger and it is thought they have less time to build up mercury levels.

METHOD

Preheat broiler or grill pan to medium-high heat. Combine Dill Olive Oil, sun-dried tomatoes, garlic, lemon juice, olives, mint, and orange zest. Mix and set aside. Coat fillets with reserved sun-dried tomato olive oil and sprinkle with salt and pepper. Place fillets in broiler or grill pan and cook for 3 minutes per side for medium-rare.

TO SERVE

Allow to rest 5–10 minutes, then place on individual plates and spoon sauce over each fillet. Garnish with fresh mint and orange zest. Serve immediately.

VARIATIONS

- Try Tarragon, Garlic, Blood Orange, Lemon, Lime, Basil, Tuscan Herb, Cilantro and Roasted Onion Olive Oil, or Rosemary Olive Oil.

VEGETABLES

GOLDEN GRILLED
CORN   90

86

SENSATIONAL
STUFFED
MUSHROOMS

SUPER EASY SPINACH
94

HAIL
TO THE
KALE

92

FARMER'S MARKET QUICHE

88

84   SPEEDY ROASTED
CHERRY TOMATOES

SPEEDY ROASTED CHERRY TOMATOES

No matter the season, roasted tomatoes always taste good. In just a few minutes, you'll have a side that is moist and flavorful and goes with most any entrée.

Serves: 4

INGREDIENTS

20–30 cherry or grape tomatoes

4 tablespoons Tuscan Herb Olive Oil

2 tablespoons Strawberry Balsamic Vinegar

3 tablespoons shallots, sliced

1 tablespoon fresh basil, chopped, plus sprigs for garnish

Salt and pepper to taste

METHOD

Preheat oven to 450°. In a baking dish, combine tomatoes, Tuscan Herb Olive Oil, salt and pepper. Mix thoroughly, spreading the tomatoes out evenly. Roast for 10 minutes, stirring one time. Add shallots and Strawberry Balsamic Vinegar, mix and continue to roast about 5 minutes.

TO SERVE

Place tomatoes in serving bowl. Add chopped basil and garnish with basil sprigs. Serve.

VARIATIONS

- Try Garlic Olive Oil and Neapolitan Herb Balsamic Vinegar for an herbaceous flavor or Rosemary Olive Oil and Black Cherry Balsamic Vinegar for a unique twist.

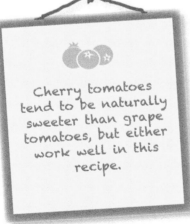

Cherry tomatoes tend to be naturally sweeter than grape tomatoes, but either work well in this recipe.

SENSATIONAL STUFFED MUSHROOMS

Fresh mushrooms are so pretty. The varieties appearing at Farmer's Markets are increasing all the time. These tender morsels can be sautéed alone, placed in soups and sauces, eaten raw in salads or stuffed like these.

Serves: 6–8

INGREDIENTS

24 large mushrooms, 2 inches in diameter, cleaned with stems removed

1 cup breadcrumbs

⅓ cup Parmesan cheese, grated

⅓ cup flat-leaf Italian parsley, chopped

2 cloves garlic, peeled and finely chopped

¼ cup Tuscan Herb Olive Oil, plus a little more to line baking dish and for drizzling

Salt and pepper to taste

METHOD

Preheat oven to 350°. Coat a large baking dish with Tuscan Herb Olive Oil. Set aside.

In a large bowl, combine breadcrumbs, cheese, parsley, garlic, salt and pepper. Mix thoroughly. Slowly add Tuscan Herb Olive Oil, mixing as you add, moistening mixture with enough Tuscan Herb Olive Oil that it holds together. Fill each mushroom to the top of the cap. Drizzle tops with a little more Tuscan Herb Olive Oil. Bake for 20 minutes or until the tops are slightly brown.

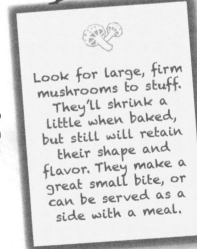

Look for large, firm mushrooms to stuff. They'll shrink a little when baked, but still will retain their shape and flavor. They make a great small bite, or can be served as a side with a meal.

TO SERVE

Place on a serving platter and serve warm.

VARIATIONS

Basil, Mushroom and Sage and Garlic Olive Oil are delicious in this recipe.

FARMER'S MARKET QUICHE

When zucchini start producing, it can be a bonanza. If you've run out of ways to prepare it, try this crust-less quiche. It can be served cut into bars as a light lunch with a salad, at breakfast, or brought to a potluck.

Serves: 6–8

INGREDIENTS

3 cups zucchini, skin on, grated — 2–3 zucchini depending on size

½ cup Mushroom and Sage Olive Oil, plus a drizzle for the baking dish

4 eggs, beaten

1 cup all-purpose flour

2 teaspoons baking powder

½ cup red onion, chopped

½ cup Parmesan cheese, grated

2 teaspoons fresh basil

2 teaspoons fresh oregano

2 teaspoons fresh parsley

Salt and pepper to taste

Adding flavored Olive Oil takes this recipe from back-in-the-day to today.

METHOD

Preheat oven to 350°. Coat a medium shallow baking dish with a drizzle of Mushroom and Sage Olive Oil. Set aside. Using a hand grater or food processor, grate 3 cups zucchini. In a large bowl, place zucchini and the remainder of the ingredients and mix thoroughly.

Pour into baking dish. Bake for 25–30 minutes or until center springs back. If top needs more browning, place under broiler for 1–2 minutes.

TO SERVE

Allow to sit for 10 minutes. Cut into squares and place on a serving dish or on individual dishes and serve immediately.

VARIATIONS

- Dill, Rosemary, Tuscan Herb, Chipotle, Green Chili, Basil, Garlic and Herbes de Provence Olive Oil add great flavor to this dish.

- Try cheddar, Swiss, or Monterey Jack cheese.

- Add red bell pepper or sundried tomatoes for color and flavor.

GOLDEN GRILLED CORN

Summertime means fresh corn straight from the fields. Cooking corn in the husk preserves its flavor and is a perfect accompaniment for a summertime meal.

Using Butter Olive Oil or other flavored Olive Oils instead of butter opens up a whole new world of flavor. If the grill is already fired up, you can easily place the ears of corn on the grill. If not, try the quick microwave method.

Serves: 6

INGREDIENTS

6 ears of corn
⅓ cup Butter Olive Oil, plus extra for drizzling

MICROWAVE METHOD

Place corn in a microwave oven on high for 2 minutes. Turn ears over and cook an additional 2 minutes or until kernels are hot and steaming. Using a potholder, place ears on cutting board and trim each end. Squeeze ear out of husk from bottom to top, leaving husks and silks behind.

TO SERVE

Place on serving plate, drizzle with Butter Olive Oil. Serve immediately.

GRILLING METHOD

Heat grill. Carefully pull back the husks and remove and discard the silks, making sure that the husks stay attached to the corn. Baste the corn with Butter Olive Oil and replace the husks. Place on the grill. Cover and turn several times making sure that the husks are completely browned on the outside — about 15–20 minutes.

Remove from heat and let stand a few minutes until they are cool enough to handle. Place ears on cutting board, trim each end and remove the husks.

TO SERVE

Place on platter or individual plates and open up husk. Drizzle the ears with a little more Butter Olive Oil. Serve immediately.

VARIATIONS

🎵 Using Chipotle Oil will give the corn a spicy, smoky flavor with a slight kick.

🍋 Lime Olive Oil will add a zesty taste.

🌿 Tuscan Herb or Rosemary Olive Oil will give it a Mediterranean flavor.

HAIL TO THE KALE

Kale seems to be king these days. And, it's not a surprise. This vibrant, green and healthy veggie contains a powerful punch of nutrients. Kale can be eaten alone as a side, in salads or smoothies, and roasted to make chips.

Serves: 4

INGREDIENTS

1½ pounds kale, washed, drained – remove stems if tough – coarsely chopped

5 tablespoons Blood Orange Olive Oil

2 tablespoons Blueberry Balsamic Vinegar

1 clove garlic, peeled and chopped

½ cup water

Salt and pepper to taste

METHOD

In a large skillet, heat Blood Orange Olive Oil over medium heat. Sauté garlic until soft, making sure it does not brown. Add water and kale and increase heat to high, stirring and coating the kale. Cover and simmer about 5 minutes.

Add salt and pepper and Blueberry Balsamic Vinegar and gently stir.

TO SERVE

Place in colorful bowl and serve.

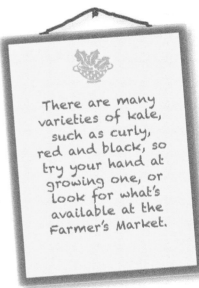

There are many varieties of kale, such as curly, red and black, so try your hand at growing one, or look for what's available at the Farmer's Market.

VARIATIONS

🫖 Scatter with fresh blueberries for color and flavor.

🔖 Try these pairings: Tuscan Herb Olive Oil and Red Apple Balsamic Vinegar, Blood Orange Olive Oil and Pineapple Balsamic Vinegar, Lime Olive Oil and Lemongrass Mint Balsamic Vinegar, or Lemon Olive Oil and Neapolitan Herb Balsamic Vinegar.

SUPER EASY SPINACH

One of the top growing greens, spinach is power-packed with goodness.

Eating spinach raw in a salad is delicious, but if you want it warm, sautéing it gently in tasty Olive Oil is the way to go.

Serves: 4

INGREDIENTS

2 pounds fresh baby spinach, washed and drained

3 cloves garlic, peeled and chopped

¼ cup Lemon Olive Oil

2–3 fresh lemon slices for garnish

Salt and pepper to taste

METHOD

In a skillet, heat Lemon Olive Oil over medium heat. Sauté garlic until soft but not brown. Add spinach and sauté until spinach is soft but not cooked through, about 2–3 minutes. Add salt and pepper to taste.

For optimum flavor select fresh baby spinach from the Farmer's Market or home garden.

TO SERVE

Place on serving platter, garnish with lemon slices. Serve immediately.

VARIATIONS

🥄 Try any one of the flavored Olive Oils for a unique flavor. Butter Olive Oil satisfies the desire for butter on vegetables without the downside. Try Garlic, Basil, Herbes de Provence, Cilantro and Roasted Onion, Tarragon, Dill or Tuscan Herb Olive Oil.

🌿 Add a few leaves of fresh basil for a flavor boost.

DESSERTS

96

LITTLE MINI
WONDERS

FINEST FLOURLESS
OLIVE OIL CAKE   **107**

100

BETTER THAN
CANDY SWEET
POTATO BARS

SUCCULENT
STRAWBERRY
DELIGHT

102

HAPPY APPLE CAKE   **104**

LAST MINUTE DESSERT

106

98

NEW SCHOOL
CHOCOLATE CHIP
COOKIES

LITTLE MINI WONDERS

These cupcakes call to mind the old, "bet you can't eat just one," phrase.
The beauty of these little mini wonders is that they're tasty and satisfying. Topping
them with a traditional chocolate glaze is anything but boring. Adding nuts, candies
or sprinkles add color and sweetness.

Makes 48 mini cupcakes

INGREDIENTS

1½ cups flour

½ cup good quality unsweetened cocoa powder

2 teaspoons instant espresso or instant coffee powder – optional

1 cup sugar

½ teaspoon baking soda

¼ teaspoon salt

¾ cup whole milk

½ cup Extra-virgin Olive Oil

1 teaspoon vanilla extract

2 teaspoons Raspberry Balsamic Vinegar

METHOD

Preheat oven to 350°. Line 48 mini muffin cups with paper liners. In a large bowl, sift flour, cocoa powder, instant espresso or instant coffee, sugar, baking powder, baking soda and salt. If you don't have a sifter, use a fine mesh wire strainer to sift ingredients. Mix dry ingredients together well.

In a medium bowl, whisk milk, Extra-virgin Olive Oil, vanilla extract, and Raspberry Balsamic Vinegar. Combine with dry ingredients, stirring until blended well.

Fill muffin cups ¾ full – about a heaping regular kitchen teaspoonful – for each muffin. Bake 10–12 minutes or until toothpick comes out clean.

Turn onto wire rack until cool, then glaze.

CHOCOLATE GLAZE

2 tablespoons unsalted butter

2 tablespoons good quality unsweetened cocoa powder

2 tablespoons water

½ teaspoon vanilla extract

1 cup confectioner's sugar

1 small jar sprinkles – optional

In a microwave-safe bowl, place butter, water and cocoa powder. Microwave 20–30 seconds until all ingredients are heated and blended. Whisk in vanilla extract and confectioner's sugar.

Carefully dip the top of each mini cupcake in the glaze, then place on wire rack to set. Once the glaze begins to harden – about 10 minutes – cover tops with sprinkles or topping of your choice.

TO SERVE

Place cupcakes on platter and serve. For later use, store in an airtight container. Cupcakes will keep for a couple of days.

VARIATIONS

🎩 Besides topping with sprinkles, try crushed candy, chopped nuts, toasted coconut or confectioner's sugar. Using candy melts takes a few more minutes, but adds color and a festive touch to cupcakes in no time.

🫒 For added flavor, use Blood Orange or Butter Olive Oil. Try Dark Chocolate, Dark Espresso or Strawberry or Raspberry Balsamic Vinegar.

NEW SCHOOL CHOCOLATE CHIP COOKIES

These cookies could become your new best favorite munchies. Make them with good quality chocolate chips, Dark Espresso Balsamic Vinegar, and Butter Olive Oil and you'll be going back to the cookie jar often. Watch the time while baking. Depending on the type of cookie sheet used, baking times could vary by a couple of minutes.

If you have any leftover, these cookies store well and retain their moistness in a sealed container for about 4–5 days.

Makes about 3 dozen cookies

INGREDIENTS

1 cup Butter Olive Oil

2 tablespoons Dark Espresso Balsamic Vinegar

1 cup light brown sugar

½ cup sugar

2 teaspoons vanilla extract

1 teaspoon baking soda

2 eggs

2 tablespoons cornstarch

2½ cups flour

10 ounces high-quality 60% cocoa bittersweet chocolate chips

METHOD

Preheat oven to 375°. In a large bowl, place Butter Olive Oil, sugars and Dark Espresso Balsamic Vinegar. Beat together until smooth. Add vanilla, baking soda, eggs and cornstarch and beat well. Gradually add flour, beating until combined. Stir in chocolate chips.

Place small scoops of dough – each approximately 1½ tablespoons – onto cookie sheet. Bake 9–10 minutes.

Remove from oven and place on wire rack to cool.

TO SERVE

Fill up the cookie jar and enjoy.

VARIATIONS

🖊 Try Blood Orange Olive Oil and Dark Chocolate Balsamic Vinegar for an intense fruity option.

BETTER THAN CANDY SWEET POTATO BARS

Who knew sweet potatoes could be made into delicious, nutritious dessert bars?
Try baking sweet potatoes in a whole new way. These yummy bars make a pretty
presentation and a wonderful treat. Store them in an airtight container in the
refrigerator for a couple of days, or freeze up to one month for later use.

Makes 16 bars

INGREDIENTS

Crust

1 cup graham crackers, finely ground – about 8 graham crackers

¼ cup + 2 tablespoons Butter Olive Oil, plus a drizzle to coat pan

¾ cup almonds, finely ground

½ teaspoon cinnamon

½ teaspoon orange zest, plus extra for garnish

¼ teaspoon salt

Filling

2 large or 3 medium sweet potatoes, such as garnet, baked until soft

3 tablespoons Maple Balsamic Vinegar

⅓ cup plain yogurt

2 eggs, beaten

1 teaspoon Pumpkin Pie Spice

METHOD

Preheat oven to 375°. Coat an 8-inch-square baking dish with Butter Olive Oil. In
a small bowl, combine ground graham crackers, almonds, cinnamon, orange zest
and salt and mix together. Add Butter Olive Oil and mix until the ingredients are
combined and crumbly.

Place the mixture in the baking dish and press it firmly to the bottom of the pan.
Bake for about 10 minutes or until set. Remove and set aside.

To make filling, remove sweet potato skins. Place potatoes in a large bowl and mash. Add Maple Balsamic Vinegar, yogurt, eggs and Pumpkin Pie Spice and blend thoroughly.

Pour the filling over the crust, smoothing the top with a spatula. Bake for 25 minutes or until the filling is beginning to pull away from the sides of the pan.

Cool on a wire rack. When completely cooled, cover and refrigerate for 2 hours.

TO SERVE

Cut into squares and place on individual plates. Garnish with orange zest.

VARIATIONS

🍊 Blood Orange, Lemon, and Lime Olive Oil work well with this recipe. Try a flavored yogurt, such as peach, pineapple, blood orange, pomegranate or apple.

🍫 Dark Chocolate or Dark Espresso Balsamic Vinegar will add depth to the flavor. For special presentation, top with whipped cream. Try baked pumpkin filling instead of sweet potatoes for a new twist.

SUCCULENT STRAWBERRY DELIGHT

The flavor of fresh strawberries is highlighted even more with the addition of the sweet-tart taste of Dark Balsamic Vinegar. Here's a quick dessert that can be whipped up and served in a matter of minutes. When fresh strawberries are not available, frozen can be used.

Serves: 6

INGREDIENTS

4 cups fresh strawberries, stemmed and sliced

⅛ teaspoon pepper

2 tablespoons sugar, if desired

3 tablespoons Traditional Dark Balsamic Vinegar

1 quart ice cream or gelato

6 fresh mint sprigs to garnish

METHOD

In a large bowl, combine all ingredients except ice cream and gently stir until strawberries are coated. Cover and refrigerate about 45 minutes.

TO SERVE

Gently stir the strawberry mixture. In individual serving bowls, place a scoop of ice cream and a large serving spoonful of strawberries. Garnish with fresh mint sprigs and serve immediately.

When strawberries come in season, the air is filled with excitement. Seeing them at the Farmer's Market or, better yet, growing on runners, is a thrill.

VARIATIONS

- Try Strawberry, Raspberry, Blueberry, Lavender, Black Cherry, Dark Chocolate or Dark Espresso Balsamic Vinegar.

- Try vanilla ice cream or any flavored ice cream or gelato such as strawberry, coffee, caramel or the flavor of your choice.

HAPPY APPLE CAKE

This updated old world apple cake is tasty enough to serve for a birthday celebration, and simple enough to enjoy with an afternoon cup of tea or as an after-school snack. It's moist, dense and fills the house with wonderful fragrance. It can be made a day or two prior to serving, and it also freezes well.

INGREDIENTS

2 cups sifted flour

1½ cups sugar

3 teaspoons baking powder

¼ teaspoon salt

4 eggs, lightly beaten

1 cup Blood Orange Olive Oil, plus a little extra to coat large tube pan

½ can frozen orange juice concentrate, thawed and undiluted, 12-ounce can

2½ teaspoons vanilla

3 apples, peeled, cored and chopped

4 tablespoons sugar

2 teaspoons cinnamon

Sprinkle of confectioner's sugar

There are so many varieties of apples at the Farmer's Market from which to choose. Granny Smith, Golden Delicious and Macintosh are always good baking apples, but why not try other varieties such as Honeycrisp, Mutsu or Pink Lady?

Locally grown apples are best, so check out what's grown and available close to home.

METHOD

Preheat oven to 350°. Coat a 9-inch tube pan with Blood Orange Olive Oil and flour. In a large bowl, combine all ingredients except apples, sugar and cinnamon. Stir, mix well and set aside. In a small bowl, combine apples, sugar and cinnamon and toss well. Pour in half the batter and layer half the apple mixture over it. Add the remainder of the batter and top with remaining apple mixture. Bake for 60

minutes and check with a toothpick or cake tester. If the toothpick or tester comes out clean, it's done. If not, bake for an additional 10–15 minutes. Do not over bake. Allow to cool in the pan for an hour, then turn onto a rack.

TO SERVE

Top with confectioner's sugar and serve.

VARIATIONS

↬ Try Butter Olive Oil for a richer flavor. Add ¾ cup chopped walnuts, pecans or slivered almonds to the apple mixture.

LAST MINUTE DESSERT

If you've ever almost forgotten dessert and need a quick, easy one in a hurry, this recipe is for you! Use ice cream and raid your refrigerator or freezer for any fruits.

Serves: 6

INGREDIENTS

1 quart ice cream

1 small bottled of flavored Dark Balsamic Vinegar

Garnish: optional

Fresh mint leaves, cherries, chopped nuts, blueberries

METHOD

Place a large scoop of ice cream in individual bowls. Drizzle a little Dark Balsamic Vinegar over the top.

TO SERVE

Serve in individual bowls. Garnish is optional, but if you have it, use fresh mint sprigs, jarred cherries, or chopped nuts.

VARIATIONS

- Depending on the fruits you choose, the following Dark Balsamic Vinegars, Black Cherry, Blackberry Ginger, Blueberry, Cinnamon Pear, Dark Chocolate, Dark Espresso, Fig, Lavender or Tangerine, are perfect accompaniments.

- If you don't have ice cream, serve berries, fresh or frozen, with a drizzle of Dark Balsamic Vinegar to bring out the flavors.

FINEST FLOURLESS CHOCOLATE CAKE

There are many versions of this flourless cake, but with the introduction of flavored Olive Oil and favored Dark Balsamic Vinegar, this cake just got a new attitude. It's so rich, a little goes a long way.

Serves: 6–8

INGREDIENTS

10 ounces high-quality 60% cocoa bittersweet chocolate chips

¼ cup + 2 tablespoons Butter Olive Oil, plus a drizzle to coat cake pan

¾ cup sugar

⅛ teaspoon salt

2 teaspoons Dark Chocolate Balsamic Vinegar

3 eggs

½ cup high-quality unsweetened cocoa powder

Confectioner's sugar to dust top of cake

METHOD

Preheat oven to 375°. Coat 8-inch round cake pan with Butter Olive Oil. Set aside.

In a microwave-safe bowl, combine chocolate chips, Butter Olive Oil and Dark Chocolate Balsamic Vinegar and microwave for 1 minute. Stir contents to blend and microwave 30 additional seconds. Add sugar and salt and stir well. Add eggs one at a time, beating with a mixer until smooth. Add cocoa powder and stir in thoroughly.

Pour batter into cake pan. Bake for 25–30 minutes or until there is a thin crust on the top. Turn cake onto a rack and allow to cool.

TO SERVE

Before serving, dust top with confectioner's sugar. Place individual pieces on plates and serve. Top can also be drizzled with Dark Chocolate Balsamic Vinegar.

VARIATIONS

🌶 This cake is delicious with Blood Orange, Lime, or Chipotle Olive Oil and Strawberry, Raspberry or Dark Espresso Balsamic Vinegar. Try Tangy Balsamic Syrup, page 16, as a garnish.

PAIRINGS

PURE EXTRA-VIRGIN OLIVE OILS **110**

FLAVORED AND FUSED EXTRA VIRGIN
OLIVE OIL PAIRINGS **111**

Whole Fruit Fused
Olive Oils **115**

Whole Herb Fused
Olive Oils **117**

Gourmet Oils **118**

FLAVORED DARK BALSAMIC VINEGAR
PAIRINGS **119**

FLAVORED WHITE BALSAMIC VINEGARS
PAIRINGS **125**

PURE EXTRA-VIRGIN OLIVE OILS

There are hundreds of varieties of pure Extra-Virgin Olive Oils available. Some of them are listed below.

Flavor intensities range from mild, medium and to robust and vary according to the variety of olive, climate, and growing conditions.

Arbequina	Koroneiki
Arbosana	Leccino
Barnea	Manzanillo
Cerasuola	Melgarejo Picual
Chemlali	Mission
Cobrancosa	Nocellara
Coratina	Oro Bailen Picual
Empeltre	Pendolino
Frantoio	Picholine
Gran Cru Coratina	Picual
Hojiblanca	Reserva Especial

All pure Olive Oils pair well with all Flavored Dark or White Balsamic Vinegars.

FLAVORED AND FUSED EXTRA VIRGIN OLIVE OIL PAIRINGS

Basil Olive Oil can be paired with the following Balsamic Vinegars:

Blackberry Ginger	Lemon
Blueberry	Lemongrass Mint
Cinnamon Pear	Maple
Dark Chocolate	Oregano
Fig	Peach
Honey Ginger	Pineapple
Jalapeño	Raspberry

Sicilian Lemon
Strawberry

Butter Olive Oil can be paired with the following Balsamic Vinegars:

Black Cherry
Blueberry
Cinnamon Pear
Coconut
Cranberry Pear
Dark Chocolate
Fig
Maple
Neapolitan Herb
Pomegranate
Strawberry
Tahitian Vanilla

Chipotle Olive Oil can be paired with the following Balsamic Vinegars:

Apricot	Dark Espresso	Pomegranate
Blackberry	Honey Ginger	Raspberry
Ginger	Jalapeño	Sicilian Lemon
Black Cherry	Lavender	Strawberry
Cinnamon Pear	Maple	Tahitian Vanilla
Coconut	Neapolitan Herb	Tangerine
Cranberry Pear	Peach	
Dark Chocolate	Pineapple	

Cilantro and Roasted Onion Olive Oil can be paired with the following Balsamic Vinegars:

Cinnamon Pear

Coconut

Fig

Honey Ginger

Jalapeño

Lemongrass

Neapolitan Herb

Peach

Pineapple

Pomegranate

Red Apple

Tahitian Vanilla

Pairing Olive Oils and Balsamic Vinegars is a matter of personal taste. Choose what satisfies your palate and flavor preferences.

Garlic Olive Oil can be paired with the following Balsamic Vinegars:

Apricot	Fig	Neapolitan Herb
Blackberry Ginger	Honey Ginger	Oregano
Champagne	Jalapeño	Pineapple
Cinnamon Pear	Lavender	Pomegranate
Coconut	Lemongrass Mint	Raspberry

Harissa Olive Oil can be paired with the following Balsamic Vinegars:

Blueberry	Peach
Cinnamon Pear	Pineapple
Coconut	Pomegranate
Cranberry Pear	Raspberry
Dark Chocolate	Red Apple
Dark Espresso	Sicilian Lemon
Honey Ginger	Strawberry
Jalapeño	Tangerine
Maple	Tahitian Vanilla

Tarragon Olive Oil can be paired with the following Balsamic Vinegars:

Coconut	Neapolitan Herb
Champagne	Oregano
Cranberry Pear	Peach
Honey Ginger	Pineapple
Jalapeño	Raspberry
Lavender	Red Apple
Lemongrass Mint	Sicilian Lemon

For a complementary pairing, choose an Olive Oil and a Balsamic Vinegar with similar flavors. For a contrasting pairing, choose an Olive Oil and a Balsamic Vinegar with individual flavors in order to taste each ingredient separately.

Tuscan Herb Olive Oil can be paired with the following Balsamic Vinegars:

Apricot	Maple
Blueberry	Neapolitan Herb
Black Cherry	Oregano
Blackberry Ginger	Peach
Champagne	Pineapple
Cranberry Pear	Raspberry
Dark Chocolate	Red Apple
Dark Espresso	Sicilian Lemon
Fig	Strawberry
Lavender	Tahitian Vanilla

Mushroom and Sage Olive Oil can be paired with the following Balsamic Vinegars:

Apricot	Lavender
Black Cherry	Maple
Blackberry Ginger	Neapolitan Herb
Blueberry	Pineapple
Cinnamon Pear	Red Apple
Cranberry Pear	Sicilian Lemon
Fig	Tahitian Vanilla

WHOLE FRUIT FUSED OLIVE OILS

Blood Orange Olive Oil can be paired
with the following Balsamic Vinegars:

Blackberry Ginger

Blueberry

Cinnamon Pear

Coconut

Cranberry Pear

Dark Chocolate

Dark Espresso

Fig

Honey Ginger

Jalapeño

Maple

Neapolitan Herb

Pineapple

Pomegranate   Strawberry

Raspberry   Tangerine

Red Apple   Tahitian Vanilla

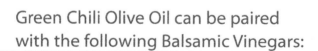

Whole Fruit Fused
Olive Oils are made
by pressing whole
fruit together with
ripe olives at the
time of crush,
creating a fresh
burst of flavor.

Green Chili Olive Oil can be paired
with the following Balsamic Vinegars:

Cinnamon Pear	Honey Ginger	Pineapple
Dark Chocolate	Neapolitan Herb	Pomegranate
Dark Espresso	Peach	Raspberry

Lemon Olive Oil can be paired
with the following Balsamic Vinegars:

Apricot	Honey Ginger	Pineapple
Black Cherry	Lavender	Pomegranate
Blackberry Ginger	Lemongrass Mint	Raspberry
Blueberry	Maple	Red Apple
Cinnamon Pear	Neapolitan Herb	Strawberry
Coconut	Oregano	Tahitian Vanilla
Cranberry Pear	Peach	Tangerine
Dark Chocolate		

Lime Olive Oil can be paired
with the following Balsamic Vinegars:

Apricot	Lemongrass Mint
Black Cherry	Maple
Blackberry Ginger	Neapolitan
Cinnamon Pear	Oregano
Coconut	Pineapple
Cranberry Pear	Pomegranate
Dark Chocolate	Raspberry
Honey Ginger	Strawberry
Jalapeño	Tahitian Vanilla
Lavender	Tangerine

WHOLE HERB FUSED OLIVE OILS

Rosemary Olive Oil can be paired with the following Balsamic Vinegars:

Apricot

Black Cherry

Blackberry Ginger

Cranberry Pear

Dark Chocolate

Dark Espresso

Fig

Neapolitan Herb

Oregano

Peach

Pomegranate

Sicilian Lemon

Strawberry

Red Apple

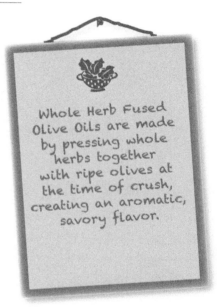

Whole Herb Fused Olive Oils are made by pressing whole herbs together with ripe olives at the time of crush, creating an aromatic, savory flavor.

Dill Olive Oil can be paired with the following Balsamic Vinegars:

Champagne	Oregano
Dark Chocolate	Peach
Dark Espresso	Pomegranate
Fig	Sicilian Lemon

GOURMET OILS

Gourmet Oils contain smooth, fragrant flavors and are perfect finishing oils. Each one has an intense flavor – a little goes a long way.

Roasted Sesame Oil can be paired with the following Balsamic Vinegars:

Blackberry Ginger

Coconut

Honey Ginger

Lemongrass Mint

Peach

Pineapple

Pomegranate

Red Apple

Tangerine

Roasted Walnut Oil can be paired with the following Balsamic Vinegars:

Apricot	Coconut	Peach
Black Cherry	Cranberry Pear	Pomegranate
Blackberry Ginger	Dark Chocolate	Raspberry
Blueberry	Dark Espresso	Red Apple
Champagne	Fig	Sicilian Lemon
Cinnamon Pear	Maple	Tahitian Vanilla

White Truffle Oil can be paired with the following Balsamic Vinegars:

Fig	Tangerine
Pomegranate	Traditional Dark
Sicilian Lemon	

FLAVORED DARK BALSAMIC VINEGARS

Black Cherry Balsamic Vinegar can be paired with the following Flavored Olive Oils:

Butter	Mushroom and Sage
Chipotle	Rosemary
Garlic	Tuscan Herb
Lemon	Roasted Walnut
Lime	

For good quality Traditional Dark Balsamic Vinegar, be sure it is from Reggio Emilia or Modena, Italy, and aged at least 18 years.

Blackberry Ginger Balsamic Vinegar can be paired with the following Flavored Olive Oils:

Basil	Lime
Blood Orange	Mushroom and Sage
Chipotle	Rosemary
Garlic	Tuscan Herb
Herbes de Provence	Roasted Sesame
Lemon	Roasted Walnut

Blueberry Balsamic Vinegar can be paired with the following Flavored Olive Oils:

Basil

Blood Orange

Butter

Harissa

Lemon

Tuscan Herb

Roasted Walnut

Remember that Flavored Dark Balsamic Vinegars are not just for salads, meats or roasting vegetables. Use them as a dessert feature, drizzling it over ice cream, cake, fruit or berries.

Champagne Balsamic Vinegar can be paired with the following Flavored Olive Oils:

Garlic

Herbes de Provence

Tarragon

Tuscan Herb

Roasted Walnut

Cinnamon Pear Balsamic Vinegar can be paired with the following Flavored Olive Oils:

Basil

Blood Orange

Butter

Chipotle

Cilantro and Roasted Onion

Garlic

Green Chili

Harissa

Herbes de Provence

Lemon

Lime

Mushroom and Sage

Roasted Walnut

Dark Chocolate Balsamic Vinegar can be paired with the following Flavored Olive Oils:

Basil	Herbes de Provence
Blood Orange	Lemon
Butter	Lime
Chipotle	Rosemary
Dill	Roasted Walnut
Green Chili	Tuscan Herb
Harissa	

Dark Espresso Balsamic Vinegar can be paired with the following Flavored Olive Oils:

Blood Orange

Chipotle

Dill

Green Chili

Harissa

Herbes de Provence

Tuscan Herb

Roasted Walnut

Fig Balsamic Vinegar can be paired with the following Flavored Olive Oils:

Basil	Mushroom & Sage
Blood Orange	Rosemary
Butter	White Truffle
Cilantro and Roasted Onion	Tuscan Herb
Dill	Roasted Sesame
Garlic	Roasted Walnut
Green Chili	

Lavender Balsamic Vinegar can be paired with the following Flavored Olive Oils:

Basil

Chipotle

Herbes de Provence

Lemon

Lime

Mushroom and Sage

Tarragon

Tuscan Herb

Maple Balsamic Vinegar can be paired with the following Flavored Olive Oils:

Basil

Blood Orange

Butter

Chipotle

Harissa

Lemon

Mushroom and Sage

Roasted Walnut

Neapolitan Herb Balsamic Vinegar can be paired with the following Flavored Olive Oils:

Basil

Blood Orange

Butter

Chipotle

Cilantro and Roasted Onion

Garlic

Herbes de Provence

Lemon

Lime

Mushroom and Sage

Wild Rosemary

Tarragon

Tuscan Herb

Pomegranate Balsamic Vinegar can be paired with the following Flavored Olive Oils:

Basil

Blood Orange

Butter

Cilantro and Roasted Onion

Dill

Garlic

Green Chili

Harissa

Herbes de Provence

Lemon

Lime

Rosemary

Roasted Sesame

Roasted Walnut

White Truffle

Raspberry Balsamic Vinegar can be paired with the following Flavored Olive Oils:

Basil

Blood Orange

Chipotle

Garlic

Green Chili

Harissa

Herbes de Provence

Lemon

Lime

Rosemary

Tarragon

Roasted Walnut

Red Apple Balsamic Vinegar can be paired with the following Flavored Olive Oils:

Blood Orange

Cilantro and Roasted Onion

Garlic

Green Chili

Harissa

Herbes de Provence

Lemon

Mushroom and Sage

Rosemary

Roasted Sesame

Tarragon

Strawberry Balsamic Vinegar can be paired with the following Flavored Olive Oils:

Basil	Herbes de Provence
Blood Orange	Lemon
Butter	Lime
Chipotle	Rosemary
Harissa	Tuscan Herb

Tahitian Vanilla Balsamic Vinegar can be paired with the following Flavored Olive Oils:

All flavored Dark Balsamic Vinegars pair well with all pure Extra-virgin Olive Oils such as those listed on page 110.

Blood Orange

Butter

Cilantro and Roasted Onion

Chipotle

Harissa

Herbes de Provence

Lemon

Lime

Mushroom and Sage

Tuscan Herb

Tangerine Balsamic Vinegar can be paired with the following Flavored Olive Oils:

Basil	Lemon
Blood Orange	Lime
Harissa	Roasted Sesame
Herbes de Provence	White Truffle

FLAVORED WHITE BALSAMIC VINEGARS

Apricot Balsamic Vinegar can be paired
with the following Flavored Olive Oils:

Chipotle

Garlic

Harissa

Lemon

Lime

Mushroom and Sage

Tuscan Herb

Roasted Walnut

Cooking with Flavored White Balsamic Vinegar adds a fresh, crisp taste. Add a little to your glass of water and enjoy a healthy, flavorful drink.

Coconut Balsamic Vinegar can be
paired with the following Flavored Olive Oils:

Blood Orange	Garlic	Lime
Butter	Harissa	Roasted Sesame
Chipotle	Herbes de Provence	Tarragon
Cilantro and Roasted Onion	Lemon	Roasted Walnut

Cranberry Pear Balsamic Vinegar can be
paired with the following Flavored Olive Oils:

Blood Orange	Lime
Butter	Mushroom and Sage
Chipotle	Rosemary
Harissa	Tuscan Herb
Herbes de Provence	Roasted Walnut
Lemon Olive Oil	

Honey Ginger Balsamic Vinegar can be paired with the following Flavored Olive Oils:

Basil

Blood Orange

Chipotle

Cilantro and Roasted Onion

Garlic

Green Chili

Harissa

Herbes de Provence

Lemon

Lime

Roasted Sesame

Jalapeño Balsamic Vinegar can be paired with the following Flavored Olive Oils:

Basil

Blood Orange

Cilantro and Roasted Onion

Chipotle

Garlic

Harissa

Lime

Tarragon

Lemongrass Mint Balsamic Vinegar can be paired with the following Flavored Olive Oils:

Basil

Chipotle

Cilantro and Roasted Onion

Garlic

Harissa

Lime

Roasted Sesame

Oregano Balsamic Vinegar can be paired with the following Flavored Olive Oils:

Basil

Garlic

Lemon

Lime

Rosemary

Tuscan Herb

Peach Balsamic Vinegar can be paired with the following Flavored Olive Oils:

Basil

Cilantro & Roasted Onion

Chipotle

Garlic

Green Chili

Harissa

Herbes de Provence

Lemon

Roasted Sesame

Rosemary

Tarragon

Tuscan Herb

For good quality Premium White Balsamic Vinegar, be sure it is from Reggio Emilia or Modena, Italy, and aged at least 12 years.

Pineapple Balsamic Vinegar can be paired with the following Flavored Olive Oils:

All flavored White Balsamic Vinegars pair well with all pure Extra-Virgin Olive Oils such as those listed on page 110.

Basil

Blood Orange

Chipotle

Cilantro and Roasted Onion

Garlic

Green Chili

Harissa

Herbes de Provence

Lemon

Lime

Mushroom and Sage

Tarragon

Tuscan Herb

Roasted Sesame

Sicilian Lemon Balsamic Vinegar can be paired with the following Flavored Olive Oils:

Basil

Chipotle

Cilantro and Roasted Onion

Dill

Garlic

Green Chili

Herbes de Provence

Mushroom and Sage

Rosemary

Roasted Sesame

Tarragon

Tuscan Herb

White Truffle

ACKNOWLEDGMENTS

Thank you to a brilliant customer, Karen Evensen, whose seemingly casual suggestion that I write another cookbook gave me the jump-start I needed.

Abundant thanks to genius friend, Jackie Willey, for expert advice in all aspects of the publishing world, from writing, editing, and proof reading to finances, spreadsheets, and marketing.

Appreciation to friend and business-woman-extraordinaire, Sandy Burn, for generosity in sharing content ideas, creative marketing suggestions and encouraging me every step of the way.

Gratitude to my son, Jeremy Jones, and daughter-in-law, Clare Hilger, for continuous encouragement throughout this project and for sharing their imaginative recipes.

Kudos to sister and Renaissance woman, Lorrie Castellano, for accomplished cooking, beautiful food styling, and for making the recipes come alive with her fancy pants photography.

Dawn Anderson

ABOUT THE AUTHOR

Michele Castellano Senac lives, writes and cooks in Greenville, South Carolina. She is a Registered Nurse with a passion for healthy living. Her love of olive oil, balsamic vinegar and fresh, vibrant foods were the inspiration for *Time After Time,* her third book.

ABOUT THE PHOTOGRAPHER

Lorrie Castellano is a Cook, Food Stylist, Photographer and occasional Blogger. She lives in Palo Alto, California, with her husband Roger and her dog Turk.

Index

CPSIA information can be obtained at www.ICGtesting.com
Printed in the USA
LVOW05s2147221015

459357LV00002B/2/P